FACE TO FACE
WITH
JESUS

RANDY ALCORN

HARVEST HOUSE PUBLISHERS
EUGENE, OREGON

Cover by Bryce Williamson, Eugene, OR

The author is grateful for the helpful counsel of the literary agency WTA Services LLC, Franklin, TN.

Face to Face with Jesus

Copyright © 2019 Randy Alcorn
Published by Harvest House Publishers
Eugene, Oregon 97408
www.harvesthousepublishers.com

ISBN 978-0-7369-7381-6 (pbk.)

Library of Congress Cataloging-in-Publication Data is on file at the Library of Congress, Washington, DC.

Printed in the United States of America

18 19 20 21 22 23 24 25 26 / VP-GL / 10 9 8 7 6 5

The Son is the image of the invisible God…For in him all things were created: things in heaven and on earth, visible and invisible, whether thrones or powers or rulers or authorities; all things have been created through him and for him. He is before all things, and in him all things hold together…so that in everything he might have the supremacy. For God was pleased to have all his fullness dwell in him, and through him to reconcile to himself all things.

COLOSSIANS 1:15-20

"Jesus changes everything about a person's life, from the obvious to the unseen. He shatters black and white into brilliant color and shakes the asleep until they're wide awake."

JAQUELLE CROWE

"His appearance from heaven will not only be the last event of the old order but also the first of the new order; further, by this appearance he will complete God's work in the old age in order to become the Center of the new age. In, through, by, and with him the End will be the Beginning and the Last will be the First. AMEN. COME, LORD JESUS."

PETER TOON

*I dedicate this book to seven of our wonderful
EPM staff members,
each of whom had a significant hand in the editing:*

Stephanie Anderson (who also helped compile),

Chelsea Weber, Doreen Button,

Brenda Abelein, Karen Coleman,

Shauna Hernandez, and Kathy Norquist.

*You have the hearts of servants,
and in each of you I see Jesus.*

Introduction

Jesus Changes Everything

From childhood I've loved astronomy. I grew up in an unbelieving home. Night after night I'd gaze at the stars, clueless about a Creator, but yearning for something greater than myself.

One night, as I stared through my telescope at the great galaxy of Andromeda with its trillion stars 2.5 million light years away, I was filled with awe. I longed to explore its wonders and lose myself in its vastness.

I read fantasy and science fiction stories of other worlds, of great battles and causes. I knew that the universe was huge beyond comprehension. But my wonder was trumped by a sometimes unbearable sense of loneliness and separation. In retrospect, I think I wanted to worship, but I didn't know what or who to worship. I wept not only because I felt so insignificant, but also because I felt so disconnected from the Significant One I did not know or know of.

Several years later, at age fifteen, after attending a church youth group, I opened a Bible and saw these words for the first time: "In the beginning God created the heavens and the earth." And then I read verse 14, the greatest understatement ever: "He made the stars also." A universe one hundred billion light years across containing countless stars, and the Bible makes them sound like a casual add-on!

I quickly realized that this book was about the Person who made the universe, including Andromeda and Earth—and me.

I had no reference points when I read the Bible. All of it was new, intriguing, sometimes confusing, and utterly disorienting. But when I reached the Gospels, something changed. I was immediately fascinated by Jesus. I'd been an avid reader of fiction, but I knew this wasn't fiction. I knew Jesus wasn't just a character in a story. I soon came to believe that he not only lived two thousand years ago, but that he still lived. Everything about Jesus of Nazareth struck me as completely believable. And, somehow, I knew he was the One my heart had always longed for.

By a miracle of grace, Jesus touched me deeply, gave me a new heart, and utterly transformed my life. Forty-five years later, he's still unveiling himself and changing me into his image and likeness. I couldn't be happier that he's every bit as real to me now as the moment I met him—but now I know him better, and therefore worship him more deeply.

For me, Jesus didn't just change everything back then. He still changes everything today.

Humble Savior

Having been raised with no knowledge of God, part of what drew me to Christ is how the Gospel accounts seemed so contrary to typical human reasoning. Yet I found them completely credible. No human would make up such a story! It had the ring of truth to me...and still has.

In the Old Testament, we read how God kept reaching down to his people: "The LORD...sent word to them through his messengers again and again, because he had pity on his people...But they mocked God's messengers, despised his words and scoffed at his prophets" (2 Chronicles 36:15-16).

The prophets foretold the coming of Messiah. Yet centuries of oppression and suffering passed, and many lost hope. In every generation there were people like Simeon and Anna who longed for and prayed for Messiah's coming. And finally, when the Redeemer's absence became unbearable, he came: "But when the set time had fully come, God sent his Son, born of a woman" (Galatians 4:4).

Jesus came to us in humility. He didn't have the honor of being born to the house of a king. He wasn't born in Rome, the world's political capital, or Athens, the philosophical capital, or Alexandria, the intellectual capital, or even Jerusalem, the religious capital. He was born in tiny Bethlehem, which means simply "House of Bread."

Jesus came in humiliation. Everyone who could count thought he was conceived out of wedlock, a shameful thing in that time and place. He grew up in a town of ill repute, where a Roman military outpost accounted for moral corruption: "Nazareth! Can anything good come from there?" (John 1:46).

Jesus worked as a humble carpenter, lived in relative poverty, and endured many indignities as he spent three years teaching and healing and speaking the good news of God's Kingdom. And then, the eternal and infinitely holy Son of God chose to endure the most shameful death—crucifixion with its excruciating suffering—to take our sins on himself. Not some, but all of them.

Who Is He?

Jesus made bold claims about his identity, which religious leaders of his day considered blasphemy. He claimed to be God's only Son, one with the Father, descended from Heaven and destined to rule the universe as King. And what response was he met with? "For this reason they tried all the more to kill him" (John 5:18).

Many today try to reduce Jesus to the role of a good teacher, one good moral example, maybe the best among many. But his own claims about himself in Scripture make that impossible. In his book *Mere Christianity*, C.S. Lewis famously pointed out,

I am trying here to prevent anyone saying the really foolish thing that people often say about him: I'm ready to accept Jesus as a great moral teacher, but I don't accept his claim to be God. That is the one thing we must not say. A man who was merely a man and said the sort of things Jesus said would not be a great moral teacher. He would either be a lunatic…or else he would be the Devil of Hell… but let us not come with any patronising nonsense about his being a great human teacher. He has not left that open to us. He did not intend to.

The battle for human souls pivots on the issue of Christ's identity. He's the watershed, the dividing line between Hell and Heaven. Jesus made that clear when he asked his disciples about his divinity: "'But what about you?' he asked. 'Who do you say I am?'" (Matthew 16:15).

That question is the most important one we will ever answer. Our own eternity hangs in the balance. Who do *you* say Jesus is? Who do you believe, in your mind and deep in your heart, that he really is? Every person must give an answer—and whether our answer is right could not be more consequential.

Come and See

When Peter identified Jesus as the Messiah, Jesus said to him, "'Simon son of Jonah, you are a *happy* man!

Because it was not flesh and blood that revealed this to you but my Father in heaven'" (Matthew 16:17 TJB).

Happy is the person who recognizes the real Jesus! It was true of his disciples then, and it's true of us now.

Biblical Christianity is fundamentally not simply a religion *about* Christ, but a relationship *with* Christ. If we get it right about Jesus, we can afford to get some minor things wrong. But if we get it wrong about Jesus, it won't matter in the end what else we get right.

The Bible reveals that Jesus Christ, God's Son, in a supreme act of love became a man to deliver us from sin and suffering (John 3:16). Jesus lived a sinless life (Hebrews 2:17-18; 4:15-16). He died to pay the penalty for our sins (2 Corinthians 5:21). On the cross, he took upon himself the Hell we do deserve in order to purchase for us the Heaven we don't deserve. At his death he said, "It is finished" (John 19:30), using the Greek word for canceling certificates of debt—meaning "paid in full." Jesus then rose from the grave, defeating sin and conquering death (1 Corinthians 15:3-4,54-57).

Christ offers freely the gift of forgiveness and eternal life: "Let the one who is thirsty come; and let the one who wishes take the free gift of the water of life" (Revelation 22:17).

Besides knowing his name, have you come to know Jesus as your Savior and Lord and best friend? "Come and see what God has done," the psalmist says, "his awesome deeds for mankind!" (Psalm 66:5). "Taste and see that the LORD is good" (Psalm 34:8).

Scripture gives us many invitations to come to God and personally experience him. Open the Bible and learn about Jesus. Set aside all other arguments and study the person of Christ. Read of his life in the Gospels, the books of Matthew, Mark, Luke, and John. Listen to his words. Ask yourself who he is and whether you could believe in him. If you hold him at a distance, you will never see him for who he is. Philip simply invited his friend Nathanael to "come and see" Jesus (John 1:45-46).

Have you come? Have you seen him? If not, brace yourself. Because once you see Jesus—I mean see him as he *really* is—you, your worldview, goals, affections, and *everything* will change. And because he never gives up on us, the changes won't stop. He's about growth not death, sanctification not stagnation. That's the key to a Christian life, and it's not boring but adventurous. Jesus, who spun the galaxies into being, paints the sunsets, and taught the humpback whales to migrate, can be comforting and rest-giving, but he is *never* boring!

Our Best Thought

Even if you *have* come and seen Jesus, accepted his invitation, and walked with him for years, you can never exhaust his depths. Puritan John Flavel wrote, "The longer you know Christ, and the nearer you come to him, still the more do you see of his glory. Every farther prospect of Christ entertains the mind with a fresh delight. He is as it were a new Christ every day—and yet the same Christ still."

There's no more worthy subject to set our minds on than Jesus himself. He is "the Alpha and the Omega...the Beginning and the End" (Revelation 22:13).

I thank God that today I don't just know and love Jesus as much as I used to; I know and love him more. That is to his credit, and I'm deeply grateful. He's what makes life so exciting and so worthwhile. Like the apostle Paul, more than ever, I want to know Christ (Philippians 3:10).

As the hymn "Be Thou My Vision" puts so beautifully, Christ is our "best thought, by day or by night." Working on this book and reflecting on the person, words, works, and centrality of Christ has been a pleasure and a joy. I hope these two hundred brief reflections will encourage you to know and love Jesus, and focus your heart and mind on him—the One who changes everything.

"I will shake all nations, and they shall come to the Desire of All Nations, and I will fill this temple with glory," says the LORD of hosts.

HAGGAI 2:7 NKJV

Who is this "Desire of All Nations," the One people long for, whether they recognize it or not? He's the Messiah, who came to deliver us.

What's he like? He's "the radiance of God's glory and the exact representation of his being, sustaining all things by his powerful word. After he had provided purification for sins, he sat down at the right hand of the Majesty in heaven" (Hebrews 1:3).

God made us, and we were made for God. It's God we long for, and Jesus, God's Son, brings the Father to us. Ultimately, God's greatest gift is himself. We need the Savior, and he has a name: Jesus (meaning "God saves").

> "He was truly God, and therefore could satisfy; he was truly man, and therefore could obey and suffer in our stead…that God and man might be happy together again."
>
> *George Whitefield*

2

The virgin shall conceive and bear a son,
and they shall call his name Immanuel
(which means, God with us).
MATTHEW 1:23 ESV

Eden's greatest attraction was God's presence. Sin's greatest tragedy was that God no longer dwelt with his people. But this all changed with Christ's incarnation. John 1:1 sets it up: "In the beginning was the Word, and the Word was with God, and the Word was God." Then verse 14 bursts forth like fireworks: "The Word became flesh and made his dwelling among us. We have seen his glory."

God walking with Adam and Eve in the garden was a wonderful preview of the God-man Jesus coming down from Heaven to live forever with people on Earth. After the resurrection, God will come down to live with his people (Revelation 21:3). Jesus is forever God incarnate.

"God became man; the Almighty appeared on earth as a helpless human baby. Nothing in fiction is so fantastic as is this truth of the incarnation."
J.I. Packer

3

But when the kindness and love of God
our Savior appeared, he saved us.
TITUS 3:4-5

The miracle of the cross was made possible by the miracle of the incarnation. The angels must have been stunned to see the second member of the triune God become a human being.

The baby born in that Bethlehem barn was God, and he was born to die. His death delivers us from our fear of death. His suffering on the cross atoned for our sins, allowing him to understand and help us.

And incredibly, the incarnation is permanent. Christ rose in a glorified human body that he'll have forever. It's not that Jesus suddenly stopped being a man after the ascension. No, the second member of the triune God will be a human being who reigns eternally on the New Earth.

> "He was created by a mother whom he created. He cried in the manger in wordless infancy, he the Word, without whom all human eloquence is mute."
>
> *Augustine*

4

And there it was—the star they had seen at its rising...When they saw the star, they were overwhelmed with joy.
MATTHEW 2:9-10 CSB

Since the wise men were so happy to see the star pointing toward Jesus, imagine their joy in the presence of Jesus himself. When they found the Messiah, "they bowed down and worshiped him" (Matthew 2:11).

Mary, Elizabeth, the shepherds, the angels, Simeon, and Anna were overcome with happiness at the Messiah's arrival, and the preborn John jumped for joy at the presence of Jesus (Luke 1:44).

This is the same Jesus who is the source of our eternal happiness. Since we're now indwelt by the Spirit of this incarnate God, who has promised to be with us always, surely we have even greater reason to experience joy!

> "You were...created for the incomparable pleasure that knowing Jesus alone can bring. Only then, in him, will you encounter the life-changing, soul-satisfying delight that God, for his glory, created you to experience."
>
> *Sam Storms*

5

When the set time had fully come, God sent his Son,
born of a woman, born under the law, to redeem
those under the law, that we might
receive adoption to sonship.

GALATIANS 4:4-5

God always knew the exact moment he would send Jesus Christ to the earth. When the gospel was manifested in Christ, God made sure the world had experienced enough of life without the Messiah to see their desperate need for the "good news of happiness" (Isaiah 52:7 NLV).

Jesus was the Lamb, the Passover, Priest, Prophet, King, the Bread of Life, the Word. Without history and the Scriptures, we would never have understood the depths of the Godhead.

God designed the world in such a way that he knew to send Messiah at *just* the right time.

> "God hath long contended with a stubborn world, and thrown down many a blessing upon them; and when all his other gifts could not prevail, he at last made a gift of himself."
>
> *Henry Scougal*

6

And she gave birth to her firstborn son and wrapped him in swaddling cloths and laid him in a manger, because there was no place for them in the inn.

LUKE 2:7 ESV

When you're traveling late at night without reservations, nothing's more discouraging than finding only "No Vacancy" signs.

Jesus knew what it was like to have no vacancy in the inn. Human logic says the King of kings should have been born in a palace, surrounded by luxury. Instead, the only door open to the humble Savior was a dirty stable. Amazingly, and revealingly, this was all by God's design.

Why is this good news for us? Because the Savior offered himself on our behalf, we won't find "No Vacancy" signs in Heaven. If we've made our reservations by accepting God's gift in Christ, then Heaven is wide open with plenty of room for all of us.

> "By his own descent to the earth he has prepared our ascent to heaven."
>
> *John Calvin*

7

*[Anna] never left the temple but worshiped night
and day…She gave thanks to God and spoke about
the child to all who were looking forward to the
redemption of Jerusalem.*

LUKE 2:37-38

After Jesus' birth, Mary and Joseph came to the temple in
Jerusalem to present him to the Lord. There they met the
hopeful prophetess Anna who worshiped at the temple
night and day, fasting and praying (Luke 2:36-38).

During this time, what were God's people looking forward to? Redemption. Their own redemption? Of course.
But also the redemption of their families, their city, Jerusalem, and even the whole earth.

The agent of that redemption? Jesus, this child, the
Messiah who would become King not only of redeemed
individuals, but also of a redeemed earth. This is the gospel of the Kingdom.

> "The total work of Christ is nothing less than to
> redeem this entire creation from the effects of sin.
> That purpose will not be accomplished until…Para-
> dise Lost has become Paradise Regained."
>
> *Anthony Hoekema*

8

"Don't think that I came to abolish the Law or the Prophets. I did not come to abolish but to fulfill."
MATTHEW 5:17 CSB

It's sobering to realize Jesus came down hardest on the very people whose doctrinal statement was closest to his own—the Pharisees, the Bible-believing faithful of their day.

Jesus compares two men who went to the temple to pray. The Pharisee's words drip with self-congratulation. He achieves status by elevating himself, pulling down others. Jesus describes the other man, a tax collector: "He would not even look up to heaven, but...said, 'God, have mercy on me, a sinner.'" Christ said he was the one who "went home justified before God" (Luke 18:9-14).

But how can the unrighteous be justified? "Abraham believed God, and it was credited to him as righteousness" (Romans 4:3). Righteousness never comes by faith in self, but in Jesus. We all desperately need him and the salvation he offers.

> "I am vile indeed, but Jesus is...an all-sufficient Savior."
>
> *John Newton*

This is how God showed his love among us:
He sent his one and only Son into the world
that we might live through him.
1 JOHN 4:9

The carpenter of Nazareth, first crying in a wooden manger, then with splinters in his hands, and finally nails in his palms, bore God's complete wrath for us—because he loved us.

It helps to personalize "God so loved the world." Christ didn't die for the world or the church in general, but for people in particular. Each believer's name is written in the Book of Life. When you are suffering most, he cares about you in particular.

God's people have always put their own suffering in perspective by looking at Christ's. Can you gaze on the crucified Christ and still resent God for not doing enough to show you his love?

> "When I consider my crosses, tribulations, and temptations, I shame myself almost to death, thinking what they are in comparison of the sufferings of my blessed Savior Christ Jesus."
>
> *Martin Luther*

10

Jesus said to him, "Have I been among you all this time and you do not know me, Philip? The one who has seen me has seen the Father."

JOHN 14:9 CSB

The baby of Bethlehem was Creator of the universe, pitching his tent on the humble camping ground of our little planet. God's glory now dwelt in Christ. He was the Holy of Holies. People had only to look at Jesus to see God, his permanent manifestation.

In *Hidden Christmas*, Timothy Keller writes, "When you read the Gospels, you are seeing God's perfections... in all their breath-taking, real-life forms. You can know the glories of God from the Old Testament, but in Jesus Christ they come *near*."

Jesus makes the Father known: "No one has ever seen God; the only God, who is at the Father's side, he has made him known" (John 1:18 ESV).

> "Christ is the delight of the Father. What solace must that soul be filled with, that has the possession of him to all eternity!"
>
> *John Bunyan*

11

"In my Father's house are many rooms...I am going away to prepare a place for you."
JOHN 14:2 CSB

Christ's birth into a carpenter's family was no accident. A good carpenter works carefully and skillfully, taking pride in his work. When he makes something for his bride or his children, he takes special care and delight.

The Nazareth carpenter had experience building entire worlds throughout the universe. But carpenters don't only create new things; they also fix broken things. Jesus is an expert at *repairing* what has been damaged—whether people or worlds. This damaged creation cries out to be repaired, and it's his plan to remodel the old Earth on a grand scale. How great will be the resurrected planet that he calls the New Earth—the one Jesus says will forever be our home...and *his*.

> "Jesus made this broken world his destination so that our final destination would be a place where every form of brokenness has ended."
>
> *Paul David Tripp*

12

For the entire fullness of God's nature dwells bodily in Christ...the head over every ruler and authority.
COLOSSIANS 2:9-10 CSB

Jesus' declaration "Before Abraham was born, I am!" (John 8:58) was a direct claim to be Yahweh, the God whose name is "I AM WHO I AM" (Exodus 3:14). We know those who heard him understood exactly what he was claiming, because "they picked up stones to stone him" (John 8:59).

In John's Gospel, Jesus makes more "I am" statements affirming his deity. The God-man said, "I am"..."the bread of life" (John 6:35,48,51); "the light of the world" (John 8:12; 9:5); "the gate" (John 10:9); "the good shepherd" (John 10:11,14); "the resurrection and the life" (John 11:25-26); "the way and the truth and the life" (John 14:6); and "the vine" (John 15:5).

Jesus, who always was, is the eternal "I am."

> "That Jesus is himself God is the heart of the gospel, because apart from his deity he could not save a single soul."
>
> *John MacArthur*

13

Rich and poor have this in common:
The LORD is the Maker of them all.
PROVERBS 22:2

When he was on earth, our Lord lived simply, but he wasn't an ascetic. He moved with equal ease among the poor, like John the Baptist and Bartimaeus, and the wealthy, like Lazarus, Martha, Nicodemus, Zacchaeus, and Joseph of Arimathea. Jesus accepted material support from wealthy women (Luke 8:2-3), and gratefully accepted the extravagant anointing of his body with an expensive perfume (Matthew 26:6-13; Luke 7:36-50; John 12:1-8).

Christ's birth attracted poor shepherds and rich kings. His life on earth drew many—both poor and wealthy. And regardless of their means, Jesus was pleased to accept into his Kingdom *all* who would bow their knee before the Messiah.

> "O Christian, never be proud of things that are so transient, injurious, and uncertain as the riches of this evil world! But set your heart on the true and durable riches of grace in Christ Jesus."
>
> Isaac Ambrose

*He exercised this power in Christ by raising
him from the dead and seating him at his
right hand in the heavens.*
EPHESIANS 1:20 CSB

Where is Christ? At the right hand of God (Hebrews 12:2).
In terms of his human body, Christ is in one location, and
only one.

But despite his fixed location at God's right hand,
Jesus is here now, living within us (Galatians 2:20). If he
indwells those who are saints and yet sinners now, how
much more will he be able to indwell us in the world to
come when no sin shall separate us from him? On the New
Earth, we might regularly hear Jesus speak directly to us in
an unhindered two-way conversation, whether we're hun-
dreds of miles away in another part of the New Jerusalem,
thousands of miles away on another part of the New Earth,
or thousands of light years away in the new universe.

"We crave deep intimacy with Jesus; and we are
most alive and free when we realize and pursue it."
Scotty Smith

And he who was seated on the throne said, "Behold, I am making all things new... Write this down, for these words are trustworthy and true."

REVELATION 21:5 ESV

In Isaiah 11:1-10, we're told of the Messiah's mission to Earth: "With justice he will give decisions for the poor... with the breath of his lips he will slay the wicked" (v. 4). He "will stand as a banner for the peoples," and "his resting place will be glorious" (v. 10). This will not happen "up there" in a distant Heaven but "down here" on Earth.

God is a promise keeper, not a promise breaker. Notice how Jesus completes his pledge: "These words are trustworthy and true." It's like he's saying, "John, you can take these words to the bank; I'll stake my life on them. In fact, I already have."

These are the words of King Jesus. Count on them.

> "Christ will by his death destroy the power of death, take away the sting of the first death, and prevent the second."
>
> *John Wesley*

*Then the end will come, when he hands over the
kingdom to God the Father after he has destroyed
all dominion, authority and power...
The last enemy to be destroyed is death.*
1 CORINTHIANS 15:24,26

What delivers us from the fear of death? Only a relationship with the person who died on our behalf (1 Corinthians 15:55-57). If we don't know Jesus, we'll fear death—and we should.

"To die will be an awfully big adventure," says Peter Pan. But a wonderful big adventure only for those who are covered by Christ's blood. Without Jesus, it's a horrifying eternal tragedy.

Death is our ultimate problem. God sent his Son to make death a passageway into the loving presence of God.

We shouldn't glorify or romanticize death—Christ didn't. But for those who know Jesus, death is the *final* pain and the *last* enemy.

"I am ready to meet God face to face tonight...for
all my sins are covered by the atoning blood."
R.A. Torrey

*The true light that gives light to everyone
was coming into the world.*
JOHN 1:9

John's Gospel tells us Jesus is the light that "shines in the darkness, and the darkness has not overcome it" (John 1:5). And Jesus fulfilled Isaiah's prophecy: "The people living in darkness have seen a great light; on those living in the land of the shadow of death a light has dawned" (Matthew 4:16).

I love John 1:9, which says that Jesus came as the light that "enlightens every man" (NASB). I think it reflects the fact that all people in history have benefited from Christ's redemptive life and death—even those who reject him. The model of Christ, his grace and truth, his elevation of women and conciliatory words, has created a reference point for bringing greater freedom and civil rights to many societies throughout history.

> "As the centuries pass, the evidence is accumulating that...Jesus is the most influential life ever lived on this planet."
>
> *Kenneth Latourette*

> *"Don't store up for yourselves treasures on earth…*
> *But store up for yourselves treasures in heaven,*
> *where neither moth nor rust destroys, and where*
> *thieves don't break in and steal. For where your*
> *treasure is, there your heart will be also."*
> MATTHEW 6:19-21 CSB

There's truth in the old maxim "You can't take it with you." But Jesus adds a new corollary, essentially, "You can't take it with you, but you can send it on ahead."

In Wall Street terms, Christ is bearish when it comes to investing on Earth. His financial forecast for this world is ultimately bleak. But he's unreservedly bullish about investing in Heaven, where every market indicator is eternally positive.

Christ's primary argument against amassing material wealth? It's simply a poor investment.

What we give in Christ's name will ultimately come back to us in a better and permanent form. He's promised.

> "Any temporal possession can be turned into everlasting wealth. Whatever is given to Christ is immediately touched with immortality."
>
> *A.W. Tozer*

19

Jesus...said, "I am the light of the world.
Whoever follows me will never walk in darkness,
but will have the light of life."
JOHN 8:12

The people Jesus spoke to lived without streetlights. If they didn't have a lamp, they groped in darkness, vulnerable to assailants. They understood what it meant to walk in darkness, desperately needing a light.

Jesus didn't say, "I'll point you to the light" or "I'll give you the light." He said, "I am the light." The only Light.

The light of Christ, shining through others, can bring us great joy. Jesus called John the Baptist "a burning and shining lamp" (John 5:35 CSB).

In a dark world, our hearts cheer when we see light. Often light is embodied in a Jesus-follower, in whom we see a secondary reflection of Jesus, the Primary Light of the world.

> "Christ is the morning star, who promises and reveals to the saints the eternal light of life, when the night of the world is past."
>
> *The Venerable Bede*

20

*Jesus Christ is the same yesterday
and today and forever.*
HEBREWS 13:8

Will the Christ we worship in Heaven as God also be a man? Yes. "Jesus Christ is the same yesterday [when he lived on Earth] and today [living in the intermediate Heaven] and forever [when he lives on the New Earth, in the eternal Heaven]." Jesus didn't put on a body as if it were a coat. He wasn't made of two separable components, man and God, to be switched on and off at will. Rather, from the point of his incarnation, he was and is and always will be a man *and* God.

When Christ died, he might have appeared to shed his humanity; but when he rose in an indestructible body, he declared his permanent identity as the God-man. This is a mystery so great it should leave us breathless.

> "That infinite God became one person with finite man, will remain for eternity the most profound miracle and the most profound mystery in all the universe."
>
> *Wayne Grudem*

21

*"Be afraid of the One who can destroy both
soul and body in hell."*
MATTHEW 10:28

Many Christians have bought into Satan's lie that it's unloving—even un-Christlike—to talk about Hell. But our Lord Jesus said more about Hell than anyone else (e.g., Matthew 13:40-42; Mark 9:43-48). So, either we're wrong, or Christ wasn't Christlike!

Jesus spoke some of the harshest words of condemnation in Scripture. When we speak only of God's love, inevitably we'll diminish or reject the biblical teaching of Hell. We must look at the complete Jesus revealed in Scripture, lest we remake him in our image, with his only attribute love. By seeing him in his holiness and love, his truth and his grace, we'll learn to see the fullness of his beauty.

> "The doctrine of Hell is not a device of 'mediaeval priestcraft' for frightening people: it is Christ's deliberate judgment on sin...We cannot repudiate Hell without altogether repudiating Christ."
>
> *Dorothy Sayers*

22

Jesus increased in wisdom and stature, and in favor with God and with people.
LUKE 2:52 CSB

Jesus was morally perfect from conception, but Scripture tells us he grew in understanding through life experiences. Incredibly, Jesus "learned obedience from what he suffered" (Hebrews 5:8). Growing and learning cannot be bad; the sinless Son of God experienced them. They're simply part of being human—his humanity was real, not imaginary.

Christ didn't suffer for us on the cross only. As a human being, he suffered throughout his life, and God used it to accomplish a staggering purpose. In that sense he became more perfect, more complete, through his suffering.

If the Father used suffering to bring Jesus to maturity, surely he can also do that for us.

> "From the foundation of the world, God knew your sufferings and declared he himself would take human form and participate in them (which means that we, too, could share in his). This is not a distant, indifferent God."
>
> *Edward Welch*

*"My food," said Jesus, "is to do the will of him who
sent me and to finish his work."*
JOHN 4:34

Our food not only keeps us alive; it brings us pleasure.
What is Christ's food, his source of happiness? To accomplish his Father's will. Theologian John Gill wrote, "Now
as food is pleasant, and delightful, and refreshing to the
body of man, so doing the will of God was as delightful
and refreshing to the soul of Christ: he took as much pleasure in it as a hungry man does in eating and drinking."

Christ wants us to, like him, walk in Spirit-empowered
obedience to God's will, knowing that what brings him
glory will bring us lasting joy and satisfaction.

> "There is hope for a ruined humanity—hope of pardon, hope of peace with God, hope of glory—
> because at the Father's will Jesus Christ became
> poor and was born in a stable so that thirty years
> later he might hang on a cross."
>
> *J.I. Packer*

24

*God is faithful, by whom you were called into the
fellowship of his Son, Jesus Christ our Lord.*
1 CORINTHIANS 1:9 ESV

When God passed in front of Moses, he identified himself as "abounding in love and faithfulness" (Exodus 34:6).
Jesus is named "Faithful and True" (Revelation 19:11).

Even when life doesn't go our way, Jesus remains faithful and works in our best interests.

Paul reminds us, "If God is for us, who can be against us?" Indeed, absolutely *nothing* in life "will be able to separate us from the love of God that is in Christ Jesus our Lord" (Romans 8:31,39).

John MacDuff wrote, "Others may have proved faithless—all other help may have failed you—all may have been but as the footsteps in the sand—but, has Christ ever failed you?"

As we walk with Christ, we'll be able to look back and say with confidence that Jesus has been absolutely faithful.

> "Be assured, if you walk with [Jesus] and look to him
> and expect help from him, he will never fail you."
> *George Müller*

25

*"I am the good shepherd. The good shepherd
lays down his life for the sheep."*
JOHN 10:11

Jesus of Nazareth is the self-proclaimed "Good Shepherd."
The Greek word translated "good" speaks of moral goodness and overall excellence.

The Good Shepherd gives eternal life to his sheep.
Christ is the only Shepherd who guarantees the ultimate
safety of his followers.

No false shepherd, thief, hireling, or wolf is any match
for the divine Shepherd. These "strangers" cannot get the
sheep to follow. Sheep respond only to the true Shepherd's
voice. They won't simply ignore the stranger, but will "run
away from him," fearing harm.

The psalmist said, because of his Shepherd, "I lack
nothing." Even in the darkest valley he would "fear no
evil"—his Shepherd was with him (Psalm 23). Jesus says
that his sheep may find total security in him.

> "In the Christian's life there is no substitute for the
> keen awareness that my Shepherd is nearby...to
> dispel the fear, the panic, the terror of the unknown."
> *W. Phillip Keller*

26

Jesus said, "Father, forgive them, for they do not know what they are doing."
LUKE 23:34

Christ told the story of a servant who owes his master millions—a debt his master freely forgives. But when that servant refuses to forgive the debt of a fellow servant who owes him much less, the king says, "You wicked servant... Shouldn't you have had mercy on your fellow servant just as I had on you?" The man is jailed until he can pay his entire debt. Jesus warns, "This is how my heavenly Father will treat each of you unless you forgive your brother or sister from your heart" (Matthew 18:32-33,35).

God takes our failure to forgive seriously! There's no sin that Christ didn't die for, so there's no sin that we, in his strength, can't forgive.

> "Whenever I realize something of what my blessed Lord has done for me at Calvary, I am ready to forgive anybody anything. I cannot withhold it."
>
> *Martyn Lloyd-Jones*

27

Jesus went into the temple and threw out all those
buying and selling. He overturned the tables of the
money changers and the chairs of those selling doves.
MATTHEW 21:12 CSB

People often say, "I like to think of Jesus as my friend, not
my master." But he's all the things Scripture reveals him
to be, including judge, friend, and master. His attributes
aren't a smorgasbord for finicky Christians to choose what
they want and leave the rest untouched.

The gentle, compassionate Jesus is also the Jesus who
drove the merchant-thieves from the temple and spoke
condemnation against self-righteous religious leaders. His
less popular qualities so outraged people that they nailed
him to a cross.

We should believe *all* that Scripture says about Jesus—
whether it makes sense to our finite little minds or not.
Only then can we avoid idolatrous thoughts about him.

"The meek and mild Jesus of progressive 'toler-
ance'...was nowhere to be found when he made
a mess of the money-changers."

Jonathan Parnell

28

"I am the gate; whoever enters through me will be saved."

JOHN 10:9

Many today try to reinvent Jesus to fit popular notions of the kind of Christ people want. It may seem narrow and insensitive to say, "Jesus is the only way to the Father."

But Jesus is notoriously uncooperative with all attempts to repackage and market him. He's not looking for image-enhancers. We're to follow him as servants, not walk in front of him as a PR entourage.

If we take one attribute of Christ—his love, for instance—and divorce it from other attributes, including his holiness, we end up worshiping our own distorted concept of love instead of the true God.

> "If God were not just, there would be no demand for his Son to die. And if God were not loving, there would be no willingness for his Son to die. But God is both just and loving. Therefore his love is willing to meet the demands of his justice."
>
> *John Piper*

29

*While Jesus was having dinner at Matthew's house,
many tax collectors and sinners came and ate
with him and his disciples.*
MATTHEW 9:10

Most sinners loved being around Jesus. He drew them out
of the night like a light draws moths. They enjoyed his
company and invited him to their parties. People sensed
Jesus loved them, even when speaking difficult words. He
was full of grace *and* truth.

After Jesus rebuked the Pharisees who were ready to
stone a woman for adultery (John 8:1-11), he could have
told the woman, "Go burn for your sins" *or* "Go and feel
free to sin some more." Instead he said, "Go now and leave
your life of sin."

Jesus didn't deny truth. He affirmed it. She needed to
repent. And change. Jesus didn't deny grace. He offered it.
He sent her away, forgiven and cleansed, to new life.

"Jesus met sinners at the table, but he did not join
them in their choice sins…And we ought not expect
Jesus to sin with us today."

Rosaria Butterfield

30

When the...Pharisees saw him eating with the
sinners and tax collectors, they asked his disciples:
"Why does he eat with tax collectors and sinners?"...
Jesus said to them, "It is not the healthy who
need a doctor, but the sick."

MARK 2:16-17

Jesus loved and forgave sexual sinners. In a culture that mercilessly stigmatized immoral women as the worst sinners, Jesus reached out and touched their lives—the Samaritan woman (John 4), the adulterous woman (John 8), and the immoral woman (Luke 7).

Sexual sin is serious, but it's not beyond Jesus' grace and power to forgive. Jesus also understands sexual temptation: "For we do not have a high priest who is unable to empathize with our weaknesses, but we have one who has been tempted in every way, just as we are—yet he did not sin" (Hebrews 4:15).

What does that mean for us? Absolute assurance and certain hope!

> "The gospel is the life of Jesus for sinners...Here the broken find encouragement, for in Christ we are righteous."
>
> Joe Thorn

"Leave her alone," said Jesus. "Why are you bothering her? She has done a beautiful thing to me."
MARK 14:6

Some people consider generous giving fanatical, but Jesus calls it love. He was so moved by the gift of the woman with the alabaster jar of expensive perfume that he vowed, "Wherever the gospel is preached throughout the world, what she has done will also be told, in memory of her" (Mark 14:9).

Love generates lavish giving. Gaze upon Christ long enough, and you'll become more of a giver. Give long enough, and you'll become more like Christ.

But no matter how much we give, Jesus remains the matchless giver: "Though he was rich, yet for your sake he became poor, so that you through his poverty might become rich" (2 Corinthians 8:9). Jesus' incarnation and atonement were the ultimate lavish gift. God's unfolding drama of redemption is the most compelling proof possible of the infinite greatness of his love.

"Extravagant grace produces extravagant givers."
J.D. Greear

John saw Jesus coming toward him and said,
"Look, the Lamb of God, who takes away
the sin of the world!"

JOHN 1:29

When Jesus walked this earth, many people didn't recognize him. They were expecting the Messiah as a powerful lion, bringing judgment on his enemies, and overlooked the passages showing him coming as a lamb (Isaiah 53:7).

In Revelation, the lamb again appears, "looking as if it had been slain" (5:6). Charles Spurgeon said, "It was as a lamb that Jesus fought and conquered...'As a Lamb,' says he, 'I died and defeated Hell [and] redeemed my people, and therefore as a Lamb I will appear in Paradise.'"

Appearing as a lamb seems a picture of weakness. But suddenly in Revelation, men are hiding themselves from the "wrath of the Lamb" (6:16). The magnificent Lamb of God is also the powerful Lion of Judah.

> "This is the solution to the world's problems? A lowly lamb? Precisely. Jesus Christ. The Lion-Lamb. What a combination of meekness and majesty!"
>
> *Steven Lawson*

33

Jesus, looking at him, loved him, and said to him,
"You lack one thing: go, sell all that you
have and give to the poor, and you
will have treasure in heaven."

MARK 10:21 ESV

What Jesus said to this rich young ruler was 100 percent loving—not an uncaring ultimatum, but an offer of treasures far beyond anything the man had dreamed of.

Jesus is saying, "You care about short-term treasures you can't keep. I'm offering you long-term treasures you'll never lose."

Jesus knew that money and possessions were the man's god. Unless he dethroned his money idols, he would never be free to serve God. Sadly, he walked away.

The timeless principle? There's a throne in each life big enough for only one. Christ or money may be on that throne. But both cannot occupy it (Luke 16:13).

"The rich ruler didn't really have money. *Money* had *him*. The man who thought he couldn't live without his money, in truth, wouldn't be able to live *with* it."
Scott Sauls

But to the Son he says,
"Your throne, O God, endures forever and ever...
You love justice and hate evil.
Therefore, O God, your God has anointed you,
pouring out the oil of joy on you more
than on anyone else."
HEBREWS 1:8-9 NLT

Hebrews 1:8-9 quotes Psalm 45:6-7 in direct reference to the Messiah. The Contemporary English Version renders the last portion, "Your God...made you happier than any of your friends."

Jesus has a gladness that exceeds that of all people (which makes sense, because he created us). If we were to ask a random group of believers and unbelievers, "Who is the happiest human being who ever lived?" few people would give the correct answer: "Jesus."

If we picture Jesus walking around in perpetual sadness or anger, grumbling and condemning rather than extending grace, we're not seeing the Jesus revealed in the Bible.

"Christ is the happiest being in the universe...He mirrors perfectly the infinite, holy, indomitable mirth of his Father."

John Piper

He was despised and rejected by men,
a man of sorrows and acquainted with grief.
ISAIAH 53:3 ESV

Jesus is called "a man of sorrows" specifically related to his sacrificial work. Does this contradict the notion that Jesus was happy? Absolutely not. Sorrow and happiness can and do coexist within the same person.

When he was headed to the cross, Jesus said, "My soul is deeply grieved to the point of death" (Mark 14:34 NASB). But this was the worst day of his life—it doesn't indicate the typical, day-to-day temperament of Jesus.

When Jesus walked the Earth, he lived with divine happiness in his past, the happiness of an eternal perspective in his present, and the anticipation of unending happiness in the future.

> "The very fact that Jesus did attract hurting people to himself shows that he cannot have been forbidding in his manner...Had he been a gloomy individual and a killjoy, he would not have had such an appeal to common people and to children."
> *William Morrice*

As he approached Jerusalem and saw the city,
he wept over it.
LUKE 19:41

An abundance of biblical passages show that God experiences a broad range of emotions. He is said to be "angry" (Deuteronomy 1:37), "moved to pity" (Judges 2:18 ESV), "pleased" (1 Kings 3:10), heartbroken (Genesis 6:6 NLT), and to "rejoice over you with singing" (Zephaniah 3:17).

Unfortunately, most portrayals of Jesus show him as rather stoic and unemotional. But Scripture says otherwise. Jesus experienced compassion (Matthew 9:36; Luke 7:13), anger (John 2:15-17), and agony so intense that his capillaries burst (Luke 22:44).

The fact that the second member of the triune God suffered unimaginable torture on the cross should explode any notion that God lacks feelings. No one who grasps this truth can say, "God doesn't understand my suffering." Dietrich Bonhoeffer wrote in a Nazi prison camp, "Only the suffering God can help."

"To our wounds only God's wounds can speak, and not a god has wounds, but Thou alone."

Edward Shillito

37

*At that time Jesus, full of joy through the Holy Spirit,
said, "I praise you, Father, Lord of heaven and
earth, because you have hidden these things
from the wise and learned, and revealed
them to little children."*

LUKE 10:21

Scripture reveals that the triune God didn't become happy for the first time *after* the incarnation.

But have you ever thought about the eternally happy Son of God enjoying happiness *as a human being* for the first time? I have to believe his smiles and laughter would have been full of delight as he marveled at his incarnation.

We view Jesus as the deity who miraculously puts an end to all suffering—and so he will—but meanwhile we need to see him as the one who understands and experiences both joy and suffering, and is committed to using both for his glory.

> "We are happy to think Christ is happy...I have found it a very sweet joy to be joyful because Christ is joyful."
>
> *Charles Spurgeon*

38

"Martha, Martha," the Lord answered, "you are worried and upset about many things, but few things are needed—or indeed only one. Mary has chosen what is better."
LUKE 10:41-42

When the two sisters from Bethany gave a dinner party for Jesus, Martha was busily doing dozens of things that needed to be done, while Mary took the opportunity to sit at Jesus' feet.

We can imagine Jesus gently placing his hand on Martha's shoulder to confront her resentment, telling her Mary chose "what is better." The reference is to food—while Martha devoted herself to preparing *physical* food, Mary devoted herself to receiving *spiritual* food. She was a single-mindedly devoted and hungry soul.

Jesus values our service less than our worship. Yet it's worship that fosters the most effective service. Despite our to-do lists, we've only one thing to do: worship him, love him, listen to him, rest in him.

"The longer you know Christ, and the nearer you come to him, still the more do you see of his glory."
John Flavel

> *"You say, 'I am rich. I have everything I want.*
> *I don't need a thing!' And you don't realize that*
> *you are wretched and miserable and poor*
> *and blind and naked."*
>
> REVELATION 3:17 NLT

In Revelation 3, Jesus rebuked the Laodicean Christians because, despite their wealth, they were desperately poor in the things of God. After exposing their spiritual poverty, Jesus offered them real treasures: "I counsel you to buy from me gold refined in the fire, so you can become rich" (Revelation 3:18).

Materialism blinds us to our spiritual poverty. Richard Baxter said, "When men prosper in the world, their minds are lifted up with their estates, and they can hardly believe that they are so ill, while they feel themselves so well."

If we have everything else in the world without Christ, we're impoverished. If we have nothing else in the world, but do have Christ, we're rich.

In the end, Christ is all that matters.

"You don't really know Jesus is all you need until Jesus is all you have."

Timothy Keller

40

*Jesus said to the servants, "Fill the jars with water...
Now draw some out and take it to the master of the
feast."... This, the first of his signs, Jesus did at
Cana in Galilee, and manifested his glory.*
JOHN 2:7-8,11 ESV

For Christ's first miracle, wouldn't you expect something earthshaking?

Why would Jesus make wine for his opener? So the hosts could be saved embarrassment and people could enjoy the wedding feast. Not a great declaration of truth; just a thoughtful act of grace.

In contrast, the very next scene shows Jesus making a whip and driving merchants out of the temple. Consumed with his Father's righteous standards, Jesus wouldn't tolerate disregard for holiness and truth.

The grace of the wedding feast still in the air, what he did in the temple courtyards was a striking affirmation of truth.

A grace-starved, truth-starved world needs Jesus, full of grace and truth.

"Christ is given to us in the plenitude of his grace,
power, truth, and love."

John Murray

41

*Jesus answered them, "Truly, truly, I say to you,
everyone who practices sin is a slave to sin."*
JOHN 8:34 ESV

Romans repeatedly states that without the transforming
power of God's indwelling Holy Spirit, we are "slaves to
sin" (6:16,17,18; 7:14,25). Slaves, by definition, have seriously restricted freedom.

But Christ came to set us free from the power of sin,
"to proclaim freedom for the captives and release from
darkness for the prisoners" (Isaiah 61:1).

Because of Christ's work on our behalf, we're free to
reject sin and its misery, and to embrace righteousness
and its joy. Then we'll experience a flood of God's grace in
our lives, restoring us to the abundant life of walking with
the One who is our Lord, King, and best Friend (John
15:13-15).

If we comparison shop between sin and Jesus, the difference is obvious. One brings misery; the other, happiness.

"To continually behold the Lamb of God is life to our
  souls and death to our sins."

William Mason

42

Jesus wept.
JOHN 11:35

God does not look fondly upon death. It wasn't part of his original design but came from sin and the curse. Death caused Jesus to weep. His heart broke for the broken hearts of his beloved Mary and Martha at the death of their brother, Lazarus.

At the time, Jesus' own death already loomed large, placing a terrible burden upon him. While he knew what awaited him in Heaven, he also knew that before enjoying Heaven's comfort and glory, he had to walk through a dark valley more excruciating than anyone before or after him would ever walk.

If we ever begin to question whether God understands or if he cares, these two words are our unequivocal answer: Jesus wept. The Savior sobbed. Messiah moaned. God Almighty shed tears. What more proof of God's heart and emotions and care and understanding do we want?

> "Jesus is God spelling himself out in language that men can understand."
>
> — *S.D. Gordon*

43

Stephen, full of the Holy Spirit, gazed into heaven.
He saw the glory of God…He said, "Look, I see the
heavens opened and the Son of Man standing
at the right hand of God!"
ACTS 7:55-56 CSB

It seems before Christ's ascension that he was not yet fully glorified, since his identity wasn't immediately apparent to those who knew him well. After Paul encountered the glorified Christ on the road to Damascus, he wrote: "Suddenly a bright light from heaven flashed around me. I fell to the ground…the brilliance of the light had blinded me" (Acts 22:6-11).

While Paul's unredeemed eyes weren't ready to behold the glorified Christ, in contrast Stephen *wasn't* blinded by the glorified Christ, but was ready to meet him face-to-face. One day, *our* eyes will also behold Jesus…and that will be the best day of our lives.

"The biggest need in your life, and in mine, is to see
the glory of God in the face of Jesus Christ."
Kevin DeYoung

Then Jesus declared, "I am the bread of life.
Whoever comes to me will never go hungry."
JOHN 6:35

Jesus spoke these words to people starving for peace and hope, happiness and significance. He also said, "I am the gate." The gate to what? To food and refreshment the sheep crave: "Whoever enters through me will be saved. They will come in and go out, and find pasture" (John 10:9).

Let's remove the blinders of burdensome, happiness-minimizing religion so we can see the appealing offers Jesus made. When he says, "I am the way and the truth and the life. No one comes to the Father except through me" (John 14:6), he's also saying, in essence, "I am the only way to the Father's true and eternal happiness."

Jesus certainly offers us more than happiness—but not less.

> "Fundamentally, our Lord's message was himself.
> He did not come merely to point the way; he said,
> 'I am the way, the truth, and the life.'"
>
> *J. Sidlow Baxter*

45

*"If anyone comes to me and does not hate father and
mother, wife and children, brothers and sisters—
yes, even their own life—such a person
cannot be my disciple."*
LUKE 14:26

Writing about this verse, Timothy Keller says, "This is
not a command to literally become hateful toward one's
family. He is calling, rather, for an allegiance to him so
supreme that it makes all other commitments look weak
by comparison."

Following Jesus is abandoning trust in ourselves, and
joyfully surrendering all we are and have to him. This, and
nothing less, is discipleship.

In 1519, Cortés and his ships landed in Mexico, at Vera-
cruz. Determined to conquer, Cortés ordered his crew to
burn their ships. His not-so-subtle message: "There's no
turning back." Christ's cause is infinitely nobler than that
of Cortés, but he too calls us not to turn back (Luke 9:62).

"All to Jesus I surrender,
All to him I freely give;
I will ever love and trust him,
In his presence daily live."
Judson Van DeVenter

46

*"If you really know me, you will know my
Father as well."*
JOHN 14:7

Not only does Jesus call God his Father, but he also extends
God's fatherhood to his disciples: "I am ascending to my
Father and your Father" (John 20:17).

We also see glimpses of this astonishing truth in the
Old Testament: Moses says of God, "Is he not your Father,
your Creator, who made you and formed you?" (Deuteronomy 32:6). Consider the ultimate cost paid by Jesus.
His cry, "My God, my God, why have you forsaken me?"
(Matthew 27:46), indicated that the perfect, loving relationship with his Father was broken. He who could only
please his Father became the sin they both hated—all so
that thieving, murderous, ungrateful rebels could enter
into an intimate, happy relationship with God!

> "Other religions invite us to worship their gods,
> allahs, creators, or metaphysical forces, but Chris-
> tianity invites us to believe in a Son and to enter into
> an intimate family relationship with a loving Father."
>
> *Mary Kassian*

47

Jesus came and stood among them and said,
"Peace be with you!" Then he said to Thomas,
"Put your finger here; see my hands. Reach
out your hand and put it into my side."
JOHN 20:26-27

The only one who did not deserve to pay for sin is the one who did. In the space of six hours, Jesus paid a qualitatively eternal price for us on the cross. The extent of that price is reflected in the permanent scars on his body, which the disciples saw and Thomas touched when the resurrected Jesus appeared.

Christ's scars will remain forever. The only one who will appear less than perfect in eternity will be the eternally Perfect One. May this move us to worship and grow deeper in our love for Jesus, calling upon his grace, remembering the marks of his love for us, forever displayed on his hands and feet.

"Christianity is the only religion whose God bears the scars of evil."

Os Guinness

48

Though you have not seen him, you love him.
Though you do not now see him, you believe in him
and rejoice with joy that is inexpressible.

1 PETER 1:8 ESV

After Jesus' resurrection, Thomas wanted tangible proof that Jesus was alive. Jesus gave him the evidence he was looking for, but also made a profound statement about happiness for those who have faith in what they haven't seen with their physical eyes: "Thomas, because you have seen Me, you believe. Those are happy who have never seen Me and yet believe!" (John 20:29 NLV).

Earlier in John, Jesus said, "For judgment I have come into this world, so that the blind will see and those who see will become blind" (John 9:39). God opens the eyes of the blind, but sometimes in judgment blinds those who can see, yet are unwilling to see the truth about Jesus.

"It is...Jesus Christ alone who makes sense out of everything in this world."

A.W. Tozer

49

The jailer...fell trembling before Paul and Silas...
and asked, "Sirs, what must I do to be saved?"
They replied, "Believe in the Lord Jesus,
and you will be saved—
you and your household."
ACTS 16:29-31

There are those who choose to reject Jesus because some of his followers are hypocrites. But this makes no sense. Many people don't live consistently with what they profess to believe. Christians don't own the monopoly on hypocrisy.

There are plenty of humble and lovable Christians. But often the attention falls on false Christians or loudmouths or hypocrites. The gospel is all about Jesus. The Jesus that Christians believe in is good, even when his followers violate his teachings.

The Bible never says you have to believe in Christians to be saved. It says you have to believe in Jesus. He's the One we're invited to come and see (John 1:46), and the only One who can save and transform us.

> "Jesus himself is the main argument for why we should believe Christianity."
>
> *Timothy Keller*

*We have a great high priest who has ascended
into heaven, Jesus the Son of God...Let us then
approach God's throne of grace with confidence,
so that we may receive mercy and find grace
to help us in our time of need.*

HEBREWS 4:14,16

To a devout Jew, the notion of unhindered access to God
is scandalous. Yet that access is ours, freely. Because of
Christ's sacrifice, God's door is always open.

In light of the work done by Christ, our sympa-
thetic high priest, we're not merely permitted but actually
encouraged to enter the presence of our gracious God with
boldness. Until God sends the Messiah to rescue the world,
or he rescues us through our death, may we approach his
throne confidently, seeking his fellowship, comfort, and
grace in our time of need...today, this very moment.

> "There is one mediator between us and God. One
> priest. We need no other. Oh, how happy are
> those who draw near to God through Christ alone."
>
> *John Piper*

51

*For the grace of God has appeared that offers
salvation to all people.*
TITUS 2:11

Human pride insists we must work our way to God. Only the Christian faith presents God's grace as unconditional, with him coming down to redeem us. That so goes against our instinct, so violates our pride, that humans never would have made it up.

Scripture makes this astounding proclamation: "God demonstrates his own love for us in this: While we were still sinners, Christ died for us" (Romans 5:8).

Jesus, the sinless one, willingly gave himself to die—not for anything he had done, but to save those least deserving. We weren't merely misguided subjects; we were traitors against the King. Yet God adopts us, makes us coheirs with Christ, and invites us to his table!

If this seems less than amazing, then we're not really grasping Christ's grace.

> "Behold, what manner of love is this…that the curse should be laid on his head and the crown set on ours."
>
> *Thomas Watson*

*For he has rescued us from the dominion of darkness
and brought us into the kingdom of the Son he loves.*
Colossians 1:13

In his life and death, Jesus is the ultimate example of humble intervention to rescue those who would otherwise perish. Christ is our rescuer. He came "to rescue us from the hand of our enemies" (Luke 1:74) and "knows how to rescue" (2 Peter 2:9). On the cross Christ put himself between us and Satan, between us and Hell. He delivered us from a horrible death, granting us eternal life.

As Jesus rescued people from eternal death, so we're to "rescue those being led away to death" (Proverbs 24:11). When we were in desperate need, Jesus rescued us from Satan, the wicked one. Likewise, we're to "rescue the weak and needy; deliver them from the hand of the wicked" (Psalm 82:4).

> "Redemption is nothing less than the rescue of helpless people facing an eternity of torment apart from God's love."
>
> *Paul David Tripp*

53

A happy heart makes the face cheerful.
PROVERBS 15:13

Scripture includes dozens of passages in which it's hard to imagine Jesus not smiling: holding children in his arms (Matthew 19:13-15), raising a child from the dead (Luke 7:11-17), making his outrageous statement about swallowing a camel (Matthew 23:23-24), and contemplating the love he and his Father have for each other and us (John 15:9).

When I wrote my graphic novel, *Eternity*, I had to decide how the artist would portray Jesus' face. Having often read the Gospels, I knew his default look should be happy. Yes, I asked the artist to portray him as sad when heading to the cross. But the man who healed people, fed the multitudes, and made wine at a wedding was, more often than not, happy!

"In the Christian life our primary teacher in the way of happiness is Christ. He is our mentor; we are his disciples. And it is by observing him…that we grow in happiness."

Paul J. Wadell

54

For there is one God and one mediator
between God and mankind, the man Christ Jesus,
who gave himself as a ransom for all people.
1 TIMOTHY 2:5-6

In Job 9:32-33, Job complains that because God isn't a man, Job can't go to him about his suffering and expect sympathy or resolution. He laments, "If only there were someone to mediate between us, someone to bring us together, someone to remove God's rod from me."

Who could lay his hand upon both God and man to connect them in loving relationship? Only the God-man, Jesus, the One who would take God's rod upon himself to pay for the sins of humankind.

In his incarnation and atonement, Christ, whose suffering far eclipsed Job's and ours, fulfilled Job's ancient longing for someone to bridge the gap between God and us.

"Before any man can think to stand before the face of God's justice…he must look to the Mediator, Christ Jesus."

Stephen Charnock

55

Jesus said, "Truly, I say to you, there is no one who has left house or brothers or sisters or mother or father or children or lands, for my sake and for the gospel, who will not receive a hundredfold now in this time…and in the age to come eternal life."

MARK 10:29-30 ESV

In Luke 8:21, Jesus said, "My mother and brothers are those who hear God's word and put it into practice," meaning devotion to God creates a bond that transcends biological family.

Jesus also said those who follow him will gain family relationships deeper than blood relations (Mark 10:29-30). I'm reminded of this when there's an immediate depth of relationship with a Christian I've just met. Many of us treasure our families, but others have endured a lifetime of broken relationships. In Heaven our relationships will be pain free and harmonious, centered around King Jesus.

"Where blood relations provide measured fulfillment, the bond of Jesus' blood brings perfect relationships that never end."

Joe Holland

56

*And let us run with perseverance the race marked
out for us, fixing our eyes on Jesus, the pioneer
and perfecter of faith.*

HEBREWS 12:1-2

Persevering requires holding steadily until completion of a commitment. At the end of his life, Paul said, "I have fought the good fight, I have finished the race, I have kept the faith" (2 Timothy 4:7).

God gives us each a race to run. Finishing well demands perseverance. Following Christ isn't a hundred-meter dash, but a marathon. If we fail to fix our eyes on Jesus, we'll either veer off course or stop running altogether. When we lock our eyes on our present circumstances, discouragement sets in. If we fix our eyes on Jesus, it will comfort and energize us, giving us a clear look at the finish line.

> "[The Savior] pours out grace for you to finish the race...He stands at the head of the course and... stretches out his arms wide in exuberant welcome, exultant congregation."
>
> *Mark Buchanan*

*Then I heard something like the voice
of a vast multitude…saying,
Hallelujah, because our Lord God,
the Almighty, reigns!*
REVELATION 19:6 CSB

In 1 Corinthians 15:22-24, Paul describes Christ's reign: "As in Adam all die, so in Christ all will be made alive. But each in turn: Christ, the firstfruits; then…those who belong to him. Then the end will come, when he hands over the kingdom to God the Father after he has destroyed all dominion, authority and power."

Most scholars agree this isn't saying Christ will someday cease reigning, but that his reign will continue after he conquers his enemies.

In the end—when God rules all and mankind rules the Earth as kings—all will be right. Rebellion will be over, and the universe and all who serve Christ will participate in the Master's joy!

> "Everywhere there's a believer on this earth, there should be a taste of the victory that Christ will bring when he comes to reign on earth."
>
> *Nancy DeMoss Wolgemuth*

58

"Whoever loves his life loses it, and whoever hates his life in this world will keep it for eternal life."
JOHN 12:25 ESV

In Matthew 10:39 Jesus says, "Whoever finds his life will lose it, and whoever loses his life for my sake will find it." Many think Jesus' primary message is that of selflessness. But in calling us to lose our lives, he's actually appealing to our desire to find our lives and save them!

Everything we give up to follow Christ is nothing without him and can't satisfy. Even if it did, it would be temporary.

One day, when he says, "Come and share your Master's happiness" (Matthew 25:23), we'll gain a new perspective. We'll see that when it came to following Jesus, the benefits always far outweighed the costs.

> "Not one man has ever sacrificed for his Lord without being richly repaid…when the cross is weighed in the balances with the glorious treasures to be had through it, even the cross seems sweet."
>
> *Walter Chantry*

59

I pray that the God of our Lord Jesus Christ, the glorious Father, would give you the Spirit of wisdom and revelation in the knowledge of him.

EPHESIANS 1:17 CSB

Since coming to Christ, I've loved theology. What I've valued most is that it helps me get to know Christ better—his person, his plans, his redemptive purposes.

Some are quick to minimize doctrine, saying things like, "All that matters is loving Jesus." But the more you know about Jesus, the more you love him. The doctrines of the deity and humanity of Christ are vitally important not only to sound doctrine, but also to loving and knowing him better.

So let's dig deep into studying our Savior, first by studying and meditating on what his Word says, and second by reading Christ-centered books by those who love him.

"If the crucified Son of God is not at the very center of everything you believe about God, your theology has lost its balance, its anchor, and its meaning."

Marshall Segal

60

*Jesus answered, "I am the way and the
truth and the life. No one comes to the
Father except through me."*

JOHN 14:6

No Christian can claim on his own authority that Jesus is
the only way to God. It's Jesus himself who claimed this.
He's either right or wrong.

Oprah said on her television program when talking
about getting to Heaven, "There couldn't possibly be just
one way." So, does Oprah know something Jesus didn't?
Or did Jesus know something Oprah doesn't? (No offense,
Oprah, but I'm going with Jesus.)

We can trust in ourselves and think, "I wouldn't send
anybody to Hell for eternity." But our opinion doesn't
matter, since we're not God! If Jesus is God, we had better
trust what he said, not what we'd prefer or what is relevant.

> "Christ is a fixed meal. It is all or nothing with his
> claims. Everyone is invited, but only you can
> decide if you actually want to eat at his table."
>
> *Carolyn Weber*

During his earthly life, he offered prayers and appeals with loud cries and tears to the one who was able to save him from death, and he was heard because of his reverence.

HEBREWS 5:7 CSB

Luke 22:44 describes Christ in the garden before he went to the cross: "Being in anguish, he prayed more earnestly, and his sweat was like drops of blood falling to the ground." The enormous stress upon him broke his blood vessels. He chose to die for our evils, to be alienated from his Father, to bear an emotional pain that exceeded even his physical misery.

Bloody, realistic imagery disturbed many who watched *The Passion of the Christ.* But Christ's very worst suffering on the cross—his bearing of sins that separated him from the loving presence of his Father—couldn't be captured on screen.

> "Jesus was in a garden, not of delight as Adam where the human race was lost, but of agony where he saved the human race."
>
> *Blaise Pascal*

62

"Here I am! I stand at the door and knock. If anyone hears my voice and opens the door, I will come in and eat with that person, and they with me."

REVELATION 3:20

If you had the opportunity to spend time with anyone, whether still on Earth or in the world next door, who would you choose? Probably someone fascinating, accomplished, or perhaps beautiful. Maybe you'd hope when the time was over they enjoyed themselves and would want to see you again.

Who's more beautiful or fascinating than Jesus? Did you choose him? The good news is he chose you. If you're a Christian, you'll be with him for eternity and enjoy many captivating conversations, *knowing* he enjoyed your company. In fact, he paid the ultimate price so he could spend eternity with you.

> "The closer we draw to the Lord Jesus…the better prepared we shall be for heaven's perfection…Fellowship will be the best of what earthly friendship merely hinted at."
>
> *Joni Eareckson Tada*

63

*And they sang a new song: You are worthy to take
the scroll and to open its seals...you purchased
people for God by your blood from every tribe and
language and people and nation.*

REVELATION 5:9 CSB

God is the Creator and lover of diversity. One day, people
of every tribe and nation will worship the Lamb together
(Revelation 7:9-10).

Christ is glorified not simply by the total number who
worship him, but because this number represents every
tribe, language, people, and nation.

Because of Jesus' work on the cross, we're all part of
the same family. On the New Earth, we'll be united in our
common worship of Jesus, and we'll delight in differences,
never resent or be frightened by them. Rapper Shai Linne
says, "Jesus made no ethnic distinctions in who he died for,
so why would his people make ethnic distinctions in who
we fellowship with?"

> "There is one race: the human race. In Christ, we
> are to be one people representing many beautiful
> ethnicities."
>
> John M. Perkins

*And they were all amazed, so that they questioned
among themselves, saying, "What is this? A new
teaching with authority! He commands even the
unclean spirits, and they obey him."*
MARK 1:27 ESV

Demons recognize Christ's absolute authority. God tells
us, "You, dear children, are from God and have overcome
them, because the one who is in you is greater than the one
who is in the world" (1 John 4:4).

Nothing must be more infuriating to demons than our
realization that if we've repented of our sins and trusted
Christ as our Savior, then the same Lord who evicted them
from Heaven dwells within us. He's infinitely more powerful. Through him we can overcome them.

The devil may be big to us, but he's small to Jesus. The
greater our God, the smaller our devil.

> "Though Satan, and the rest of his apostate spirits,
> are powerful, when compared with us; yet, if put
> in competition with the Almighty, they are as weak
> as the smallest worms."
>
> *George Whitefield*

65

*He who did not spare his own Son, but gave him
up for us all—how will he not also, along with him,
graciously give us all things?*

ROMANS 8:32

The God who gave us his Son delights to graciously give us "all things." These "all things" are in addition to Christ, but never *instead* of him—they come, Scripture tells us, "along with him." If we didn't have Christ, we'd have nothing. But because we have Christ, we have everything.

Asaph says, "Whom have I in heaven but you? And earth has nothing I desire besides you" (Psalm 73:25). This may seem an overstatement—there's *nothing* on Earth this man desires but God? But Asaph is affirming the central desire of our hearts is for God.

And when we realize what it means to have Jesus, we'll never be disappointed.

> "There is only one Being who can satisfy the last aching abyss of the human heart and that is the Lord Jesus Christ."
>
> *Oswald Chambers*

But we know that when Christ appears, we shall be like him, for we shall see him as he is.

1 John 3:2

Christ's resurrection body is the prototype for our heavenly bodies (1 Corinthians 15:48-49). Whatever was true of his resurrection body will presumably be true of us.

Jesus wasn't always immediately recognized (John 20:15), suggesting there was change in his appearance. But after some time, his disciples recognized him (Luke 24:31). This may suggest despite any outward changes, the inner identity of people shines through.

Through locked doors Christ suddenly appeared to the disciples (John 20:19). Christ could be touched and consume food, yet his body could "materialize" too. How? Could a resurrection body be structured to allow its molecules to pass through solid materials or suddenly become visible or invisible? Though we know Christ could do these things, we're not explicitly told we'll be able to. Perhaps his divine nature makes this unique.

"The resurrection of Christ is the Amen of all his promises."

John Boys

He will swallow up death forever;
and the Lord GOD will wipe away
tears from all faces.
ISAIAH 25:8 ESV

David asked God, "List my tears on your scroll—are they not in your record?" (Psalm 56:8). David believed his suffering mattered, that God counted it as precious, so precious that the Lord kept track of every tear.

This gives special meaning to the promise that God will wipe away every tear from his children's eyes. We're again promised in Revelation 7:17: "God will wipe away every tear from their eyes." This means God's hands will touch the face of each child, removing every tear.

Remember, God not only made tear ducts but *has them*. Jesus as the God-man shed tears (John 11:35).

When Jesus wipes away tears with his gentle, omnipotent hand, I believe our eyes will fall on the scars that made our suffering his so that his eternal joy could become ours.

"A Jesus who never wept could never wipe away my tears."

Charles Spurgeon

68

*"God makes you happy when people say wrong things
about you, when they trouble you, and when they
say all kinds of lies about you."*
MATTHEW 5:11 WE

Scholars agree that a common meaning of *makarios* is
"happy." When it's translated "blessed," the astounding
paradox Jesus expresses in the beatitudes—that those who
know him can experience happiness amidst difficulty—is
hard to see. Jesus' use of paradox is precisely what made his
words so paradigm-shifting. Missing the startling nature
of his words misses his meaning.

How can the poor and the mourning be *happy*? Jesus
said one day, the poor in spirit will inherit God's Kingdom,
and the mourners will be comforted (Matthew 5:3-4).

> "'*Happy* are they'—there is something in the sound
> of it which arrests our attention at once, that...
> arrested the attention of the hearers of Jesus on that
> day long ago when he spoke these blessed words.
> For all the world is seeking for this gift of happiness."
> *G. Campbell Morgan*

69

*And we know that in all things God works
for the good of those who love him...For those God
foreknew he also predestined to be conformed
to the image of his Son.*
ROMANS 8:28-29

In Romans 8:29, Paul explains how he knows God works everything together for good. We usually define good by what brings pleasure. God defines it by what makes us more like Jesus.

We don't become fully Christlike the moment we're born again. God gradually conforms us to the image of Christ. In 2 Corinthians 3:18, Paul says: "We all...are being transformed into his image with ever-increasing glory, which comes from the Lord."

Often, God uses suffering to bring us back to Christ. When we're thinking clearly, we realize there's no greater good than becoming more like him.

> "God does not accept me just as I am; he loves me despite how I am...He loves me enough to devote my life to renewing me in the image of Jesus."
> *David Powlison*

*God raised him from the dead so that he will never
be subject to decay. As God has said, "I will give you
the holy and sure blessings promised to David."*

Acts 13:34

One Bible student told me he couldn't believe the risen
Christ might have DNA. But why *not*? Who created
DNA? Christ explicitly said that his body was of flesh and
bones (Luke 24:39), which have DNA. There's no reason
to believe that his new body doesn't have it.

Is Christ a former descendant of Abraham and David,
or is the glorified Christ in Heaven still their descendant? I believe his claim to rulership in the Millennium
and on the New Earth depends in part on the fact that
he remains—and will always remain—an actual, physical
descendant of humans.

> "[Christ's resurrection] is not a matter of a 'spirit
> appearance,' but the utterly unprecedented, unique,
> world-transforming, heaven-anticipating, sovereign
> action of the Creator in the first installment of remak-
> ing the world."
>
> *Bruce Milne*

*In the beginning was the Word, and the Word
was with God, and the Word was God.*
JOHN 1:1

Before time, the Father, Son, and Holy Spirit coexisted.
We see more evidence of this throughout John. In John
8, Jesus says, "Before Abraham was, I *am*." It's significant that he doesn't say, "I existed *before* Abraham," but "I
am," because he's taking on the name of Yahweh—"I AM
WHO I AM"—words God used when he revealed himself
to Moses (Exodus 3:14). Jesus was stating that as the Son
of God, he was God—the eternal, preexistent God of the
Old Testament.

Jesus isn't a created being. He's the infinite, eternal,
never-brought-into-existence God.

> "When the Bible says that Christ is God, it does not
> ask us to forget a single thing that it has said about
> the stupendous majesty of God. No, it asks us to
> remember every one of those things in order that
> we may apply them all to Jesus Christ."
>
> *J. Gresham Machen*

72

*Jesus stood up and cried out, "If anyone thirsts,
let him come to me and drink."*
JOHN 7:37 ESV

The world is full of people thirsting for meaning. In their quest, they eagerly drink from contaminated sources of water, believing it will satisfy. What they desperately long for can be found only in the "fountain of living waters"— Christ (Jeremiah 2:13 ESV).

Imagine people dying of thirst, frantically digging cisterns that can't hold water. Driven mad by the scorching sun, they shovel sand into their mouths, choking as they die. And all the while there's a spring of cold, life-giving water nearby.

Every attempt to find life other than in Christ is meaningless. We must spend time with Jesus and consume the life-giving bread and water of his being. Only then will we be satisfied and transformed.

> "We were made for a better place and for a better person...We crave Christ. He has made this restoration possible and offers himself to mankind as Savior, Redeemer, and Restorer."
>
> *Steve DeWitt*

Then Jesus looked steadily at his disciples and said…
"How happy are you who weep now, for you
are going to laugh!"
LUKE 6:20-21 PHILLIPS

One of Satan's great lies is that God is joyless and humorless, whereas Satan brings pleasure and satisfaction. In fact, it's Satan who's humorless. Sin didn't bring him joy; it forever stripped him of joy.

In contrast, envision Jesus with his disciples. If you can't picture Jesus teasing and laughing with them, you need to reevaluate your theology of creation and incarnation. We need a biblical theology of humor that prepares us for an eternity of celebration, spontaneous laughter, and overflowing joy.

The new universe will ring with laughter. Am I just speculating? No. Jesus himself says, "You are going to laugh" (Luke 6:21 PHILLIPS).

Surely Jesus will join in the laughter—and be the source of much of it. And when Jesus laughs, it's always the laughter of both God and man.

"Joy is the serious business of Heaven."

C.S. Lewis

74

And whatever you do, whether in word or deed,
do it all in the name of the Lord Jesus, giving thanks to
God the Father through him.
COLOSSIANS 3:17

When we pursue Christ, we must be motivated by something much higher than legalism or mere duty. Obligation may push us, but Jesus pulls us. We'll want to follow him when we realize he's greater than any lesser alternatives.

When I contemplate Christ—when I meditate on his unfathomable love and grace—I lose myself in him. When he's the center of my thinking, I stop worrying without trying. I become happy without trying.

We become more Christlike only as we take pains to focus our gaze on Christ. As we meditate on him and his Word, we become increasingly like him (2 Corinthians 3:18).

> "It seems to me that we ought to be unconscious of ourselves, and that the nearer we get to Christ the more we shall be taken up with him."
> *Elizabeth Prentiss*

75

He had to be made like them, fully human in every way, in order that he might become a merciful and faithful high priest in service to God.

HEBREWS 2:17

Human beings laugh. Scripture never directly states Jesus laughed, but that doesn't mean he didn't. Did Jesus not breathe or sneeze either, since those aren't stated? No, we can assume these things because Scripture says he was "fully human in every way."

Jesus didn't sin or make foolish decisions, but did he ever fall or spill his milk? He was a carpenter by trade, so surely he got splinters while working with wood. I doubt he complained, but I believe he marveled at his humanity, having brought not only God's grace and truth into the world but also God's happiness, delight, and laughter.

> "It is impossible to contemplate the character of Jesus, with serious and devout attention, and not be charmed with it. We see in him all the human passions in the highest perfection."
>
> *John Fawcett*

"I have earnestly desired to eat this Passover with you before I suffer. For I tell you I will not eat it until it is fulfilled in the kingdom of God."
LUKE 22:15-16 ESV

Jesus promised we'd eat with him in his Kingdom. How truly magnificent! To eat a meal with Jesus will be to eat a meal with God. The fascinating God is by far the most interesting person we'll ever meet in Heaven.

Imagine what it'd be like to walk with Jesus, as the disciples did. If you know Christ, you'll have that opportunity on the New Earth.

The good news is we can get to know God now. We do this when we come before him in prayer and confession, read his Word, and gather together in Bible-teaching churches with other Jesus followers.

> "To know Jesus is the shortest description of true grace; to know him better is the surest mark of growth in grace; to know him perfectly is eternal life."
>
> *John Newton*

Our mouths were filled with laughter,
our tongues with songs of joy…
The LORD has done great things for us,
and we are filled with joy.
PSALM 126:2-3

We don't have depictions of the disciples and Jesus sitting around campfires telling stories or teasing. But I'm certain they did, because *that's what people do.* Jesus knew there's "a time to weep and a time to laugh" (Ecclesiastes 3:4). Surely we should believe he did!

Growing up in a faithful Jewish family, Jesus would have enjoyed many feasts, holidays, and the weekly Sabbath, all celebratory experiences. Psalm 126, with its depictions of joy and laughter, is one the Jewish people would have sung on their way to one of the major festivals.

Laughter isn't only a human response, it's biblical and pleasing to God. It's therefore inconceivable that Jesus didn't laugh.

> "If there is a single person within the pages of the Bible that we can consider to be a humorist, it is without doubt Jesus."
>
> *Leland Ryken*

78

*"I have come into the world as light, so that whoever
believes in me may not remain in darkness."*
JOHN 12:46 ESV

During Christ's transfiguration, his clothing "became as
bright as a flash of lightning" (Luke 9:29). In Acts 9, Saul
of Tarsus was blinded by him.

God himself will be the light for the New Jerusalem.
Isaiah says, "For the LORD will be your everlasting light"
(60:19). John says further, "And the Lamb is its lamp"
(Revelation 21:23). He saw what Isaiah couldn't: the city's
light is the Messiah himself.

Christ will forever remain human, but his once veiled
deity will shine through. The day is coming when Christ
the God-man will be the ultimate image-bearer, fully con-
veying the brightness of the Almighty.

"Our bodily senses will be restored and glorified in
a way we cannot now understand, in order that we
may be able to look at Christ and his glory forever…
That glory will be a thousand times more than anything we can imagine."

John Owen

"I am the vine; you are the branches. If you remain in me and I in you, you will bear much fruit; apart from me you can do nothing."

JOHN 15:5

John Bloom says, "We are strange 'branches' that are prone to wander. Staying put in the vine is something we must obey. So why are we prone to leave the 'vine' we love? Because we are easily deceived into believing that *we* are vines, not branches."

Whether we write, build, draw, or make things— whatever we do—Jesus wants us to yield our gifts to him and depend on him for the next breath. It's imperative we trust in Christ, lean on him, and draw upon him for power. Charles Hummel wrote, "The root of all sin is self-sufficiency."

Walk with Jesus today. Call upon his grace. He's the vine; we're the branches. Apart from him, we can do nothing.

"Apart from Jesus Christ, we do not know what is our life, nor our death, nor God, nor ourselves."

Blaise Pascal

80

For you will not abandon my soul to Sheol,
or let your holy one see corruption.
PSALM 16:10 ESV

Despite Jesus' agony, he promised the thief on the cross that Heaven awaited him: "Truly I tell you, today you will be with me in paradise" (Luke 23:43). This proves that at death we enter God's presence immediately and that Jesus went to his Father upon death.

It's normally assumed Jesus' body initially remained in the tomb, just as ours will. He went into the Father's presence, and three days later the Spirit resurrected his body, just as ours will be (Colossians 1:18). The difference is Jesus' body didn't decay (Psalm 16:10).

> "The thief had nails through both hands, so that he could not work; and a nail through each foot, so that he could not run errands for the Lord; he could not lift a hand or a foot toward his salvation, and yet Christ offered him the gift of God; and he took it."
> *D.L. Moody*

81

*"And surely I am with you always,
to the very end of the age."*
MATTHEW 28:20

I encourage you to think of Jesus as your mentor and best friend, as well as Savior and Lord. Your relationship with Jesus grows as you spend time with him—as you talk and listen to him.

Occasionally when I'm praying, I pull out a chair for Jesus and envision him sitting there. I talk to him. I'm not pretending Jesus is with me when I pray; I believe his promise that he's really with me and I act in keeping with it.

We can't spend time with many of the world's famous people, but I have a hunch we'd be disappointed if we could. We can, however, spend time with Jesus daily—hour by hour. To "pray continually" (1 Thessalonians 5:17) is not an impossible chore but an ongoing delight.

> "The best advice I can give you: Look unto Jesus, beholding his beauty in the written Word."
>
> *John Newton*

*The reason the Son of God appeared was to
destroy the devil's work.*

1 JOHN 3:8

Satan's work is evil and suffering. From the beginning, God planned that his Son should deal the death blow to Satan, evil, and suffering; reverse the Curse; redeem a fallen humanity; and repair a broken world.

What Jesus did about evil and suffering was so great and unprecedented that it shook the angelic realm's foundation. It ripped in half, from the top down, not only the temple curtain but also the fabric of the universe itself.

Scripture says that Jesus, "having disarmed the powers and authorities...made a public spectacle of them, triumphing over them by the cross" (Colossians 2:15). Jesus' triumph ensured Satan's defeat; only the execution of Satan's sentence remains (Revelation 20:10).

What more can we ask from Jesus than what he's done for us and what he promises he will yet do?

> "'Immanuel, God with us.' It is hell's terror. Satan trembles at the sound of it."
>
> *Charles Spurgeon*

83

*"So do not worry, saying, 'What shall we eat?'
or 'What shall we drink?'...But seek first his
kingdom and his righteousness, and all these
things will be given to you as well."*

MATTHEW 6:31,33

Long ago there was a stress expert who never charged for
his lectures and whose convention centers were dusty roads
and countryside fields. Though many have tried, nobody's
ever improved on his advice in Matthew 6.

We should trust Jesus with our immediate futures
as much as we trust him with our eternal futures. Not
worrying doesn't erase bad things from life, but Jesus will
lessen their weight upon us as he carries the load (Matthew 11:28-30).

Following Christ means "casting all your cares on him,
because he cares about you" (1 Peter 5:7 csb). His heart is
infinitely big and his shoulders are infinitely broad.

> "I don't worry over the future,
> for I know what Jesus said;
> so today I'll walk beside him,
> for he knows what is ahead."
>
> *Ira Stanphill*

You will fill me with joy in your presence,
with eternal pleasures at your right hand.
PSALM 16:11

In the first-ever gospel message of the newborn church, Peter preached that Psalm 16 is about Christ: "David said about him: 'I saw the Lord always before me. Because he is at my right hand, I will not be shaken. Therefore my heart is *glad* and my tongue *rejoices*...You will *fill me with joy* in your presence'" (Acts 2:25-28, emphasis added). This is a triple affirmation of Christ's happiness!

The New Life Version of Psalm 16:11 says, "Being with You is to be full of joy. In Your right hand there is happiness forever."

The Christ who indwells us now is the same Christ who will bring us joy throughout eternity.

> "We shall be forever with Christ! The presence of Jesus will dissipate all gloom, disperse all slavish fears...deliver from all sorrow...and fill us with unspeakably glorious joy."
>
> *James Smith*

> *"The Son of Man came eating and drinking, and*
> *they say, 'Look at him! A glutton and a drunkard,*
> *a friend of tax collectors and sinners!'"*
> MATTHEW 11:19 ESV

The endless rules of first-century Pharisaism often negated the joy God intended through feasts, Sabbath, and everyday life. Jesus stood in stark contrast to "holy people." Serious rabbis weren't in danger of being accused of gluttony and drunkenness because they never attended parties. They probably didn't get invited! Jesus wasn't serious enough for them, so he wasn't considered holy.

Jesus came to share the good news with the poor and oppressed (Luke 4:18-19). Of course, the gospel is also for the rich and "socially accepted." But sinners and social outcasts understand bondage enough to appreciate deliverance. They understand their spiritual need, because it's not buried under layers of acceptance and prosperity.

> "Think of how happy those on the fringes of society would have been to be included in the community. The joy around the table was magnified by their gratitude."
>
> *James Martin*

86

*"I am the root and the descendant of David,
the bright morning star."*
REVELATION 22:16 ESV

Jesus refers to himself as the morning star and promises his followers he'll give them the morning star (Revelation 2:28).

In ancient literature and today, Venus is often referred to as the morning star. While other planets can appear in the sky, Venus appears consistently and brighter than others.

Why is this title given to Christ? I think it relates to hope and his imminent second coming. When Venus rises, the sun follows soon. Christ's coming means God's light is about to shine forever, fulfilling Revelation 21–22, with the creation of a New Heaven and a New Earth.

On a long dark night, the appearance of the morning star means daybreak is imminent. Jesus, the true morning star, means the eternal morning will soon dawn. What great promise and hope!

> "O Jesus, grant the gift to see
> The treasure that you are,
> And as the night eclipses me,
> O be my Morning Star."
>
> *John Piper*

87

*"I will follow you, Lord; but first let me go back and
say goodbye to my family." Jesus replied, "No one
who puts a hand to the plow and looks back is
fit for service in the kingdom of God."*
LUKE 9:61-62

Human nature hasn't changed from the first century to
now. Christ still calls people to follow him, and people still
give excuses. Their reasons may appear sound, but any reason not to follow Christ is a bad one. Delayed obedience
is disobedience.

Taking up our cross and following Jesus doesn't mean
saving ourselves but accepting Christ's atonement. He
calls us to deny ourselves, make real sacrifices, and follow
him (Luke 9:23).

Sacrifices are a temporary death leading to eternal life.
Whatever we lose serving Jesus, we'll regain a trillion times
in eternity.

"There is no other way except the way of the cross…
He simply said, 'If you want to be my disciple…'
and that stands just exactly the same way today."
Elisabeth Elliot

Very early in the morning...Jesus got up,
left the house and went off to a solitary place,
where he prayed.
MARK 1:35

After the apostles returned from ministering to people, Jesus said to them, "Come with me by yourselves to a quiet place and get some rest" (Mark 6:31).

Jesus knew there was a time to work and a time to rest. He prescribed rest for his disciples knowing their needs even when they didn't. He himself took time to talk with his Father.

It's ironic it takes such effort to set aside time for rest with God. For many of us, myself included, it's difficult to guard our schedules. But it's worth it. Our rest points us to Jesus, who says, "Come to me, all you who are weary... and I will give you rest" (Matthew 11:28).

"Jesus, I am resting, resting in the joy of what Thou art;
I am finding out the greatness of Thy loving heart."
Jean Sophia Pigott

89

*Then Jesus said to his disciples, "Whoever wants to
be my disciple must deny themselves and take up
their cross and follow me."*

MATTHEW 16:24

Our prayers and expectations for Jesus usually involve
making our lives easy. But Jesus isn't our genie who grants
our wishes. While he sometimes doesn't give us what we
want, he *always* gives us what we need.

Until we regard suffering as our calling, as Jesus did,
we'll not be able to face it like him: "Consider him who
endured such opposition from sinners, so that you will not
grow weary and lose heart" (Hebrews 12:3).

Following Christ requires daily cross-bearing. Those
who carry a cross are best able to share with others the
God-man who died on the cross. We'll bring glory to God
and can look forward to lasting reward and happiness.

"What our Lord said about cross-bearing and obedience is not in fine type. It is in bold print on the
face of the contract."

Vance Havner

"For whoever wants to save their life will lose it, but whoever loses their life for me will find it."
MATTHEW 16:25

We're called to give up everything to seek Jesus (Matthew 13:44). The rewards are immense, now and later. Whoever does what he wants will lose his life, while whoever loses his life for Christ *finds it*.

Jim Elliot said, "He is no fool who gives what he cannot keep to gain what he cannot lose." Some see this as a statement of great sacrifice. But Jim is saying it would be foolish not to give away what he couldn't keep when he would forever gain something far better.

Jesus appealed to the interest of our ultimate happiness by encouraging us to make small temporary sacrifices to achieve large eternal gain.

> "If you cling to your own plans and desires, you will never discover the freedom and joy found in losing your life for Jesus."
>
> *Nancy Guthrie*

91

The LORD foils the plans of the nations;
he thwarts the purposes of the peoples.
But the plans of the LORD stand firm forever,
the purposes of his heart through all generations.

PSALM 33:10-11

Christ's followers should want to come down on "the wrong side of history"—at least our more recent history that unashamedly celebrates evil. Given the larger picture of God's sovereign rule and the eventual New Heavens and New Earth, history will ultimately vindicate God's Word and God's Son. Therefore, when evil is popularly accepted, following current cultural trends puts us on the wrong side of God's plan of redemptive history.

"Christ is the final, complete, dominant, visible, manifest Lord of history," John Piper says. "I want to be on *that* side."

> "As Christians we are tempted to make unnecessary concessions to those outside the faith. We give in too much…We must show our Christian colors if we are to be true to Christ—we can't remain silent or concede everything away."
>
> C.S. Lewis

92

"Why do you call me 'Lord, Lord,' and not do what I tell you?"
LUKE 6:46 ESV

God is not a genie, under our control. He's the master. When we imagine ourselves as masters, it can be intimidating to agree to be a servant. Christ is in charge of the universe whether or not we acknowledge him—but when we do, we honor him by submitting to his lordship.

Jesus said, "If you love me, keep my commands" (John 14:15). We must not fool ourselves. He will not be comforted by the fact that we call him "Savior" when we refuse to follow him as Lord.

Christ must be Lord over our whole lives—including over our houses, cars, vocations, hobbies, social media, money, television, and anything else. We need to look at everything in our lives and ask, "Is this under the lordship of Christ?"

> "Jesus is not on a side. Jesus IS a side. Nobody owns him. He owns us."
>
> *Janie B. Cheaney*

Then I heard a loud voice in heaven say:
"Now have come the salvation and the power
and the kingdom of our God, and the
authority of his Messiah.
For the accuser of our brothers and sisters,
who accuses them before our God day and night,
has been hurled down."

REVELATION 12:10

Jesus is our defense attorney: "My dear children, I write this to you so that you will not sin. But if anybody does sin, we have an advocate with the Father—Jesus Christ, the Righteous One" (1 John 2:1). Christ is the Judge's son and has paid fully for our sin. In him, we're completely cleansed.

Do you rejoice knowing this? Imagine Jesus standing between you and your accuser, Satan. The thought makes me smile, rejoice, and praise God!

> "If we cannot claim to live sinless lives, then the only thing that can keep us from despairing before a holy God is that we have an Advocate in heaven and he pleads our case not on the basis of our perfection but of his propitiation."
>
> *John Piper*

94

*"Come to me, all you who are weary and burdened,
and I will give you rest."*
MATTHEW 11:28

Many hear God say, "Do more and better." But not, "I've
done it for you—rest."

Yet this is what Jesus meant when he said, "Take my
yoke upon you and learn from me...For my yoke is easy
and my burden is light" (Matthew 11:29-30).

Jesus invites us to come to him, the Source of happiness, and sit at the feet of him who wired us to want happiness. He invites us, even in this world full of suffering,
to find in him the happiness, peace, and rest we long for.

When we search for happiness apart from Christ, we
find loneliness and misery. When we focus on Jesus and
others, we find untold happiness.

> "If you can cry out to Jesus, he will joyfully hear you.
> If you will give him no rest, he will give you all the
> rest you need."
>
> *Charles Spurgeon*

95

Follow my example, as I follow
the example of Christ.
1 Corinthians 11:1

Jesus understood the importance of example. In his three years of earthly ministry, he invested deeply in his twelve closest disciples, who lived life alongside him.

It's not surprising that Scripture calls us to imitate Christ (1 Peter 2:21). It's more surprising that we're told to follow the examples of godly people around us, and to strive to be such examples ourselves (Philippians 3:17).

That's one reason it's vital to become part of a Bible-believing local church. As imperfect as we all are, by becoming actively involved in the church, we can learn from the example of others—and be examples ourselves.

It's also helpful to read biographies of faithful believers. Compare reading a biography of Amy Carmichael to watching a sitcom. Which will point us to Christ? Let's take our eyes off celebrities and put them on Jesus-followers.

"Disciple*ship* is my following Jesus. Discipl*ing* is me helping someone else follow Jesus."

Mark Dever

96

God chose what is low and despised in the world...
so that no human being might boast in the
presence of God.
1 CORINTHIANS 1:28-29 ESV

Jesus came to preach good news to the poor and needy (Luke 4:18-19). Christ takes personally how we treat the poor: "For I was hungry and you gave me something to eat...Truly I tell you, whatever you did for one of the least of these brothers and sisters of mine, you did for me" (Matthew 25:34,40).

Jesus died for every person of every social and economic level. Paul reminds the proud Corinthians that the church is made up of the dregs of this world. Elitism boosts our egos by making us think we're worthier than others. Few things are more repugnant to the Lord than the rich despising the poor.

"Christianity is not about building an absolutely secure little niche in the world...Christianity is about learning to love like Jesus loved, and Jesus loved the poor and Jesus loved the broken."

Rich Mullins

> *"O Jerusalem, Jerusalem, the city that kills the*
> *prophets and stones those who are sent to it! How*
> *often would I have gathered your children together*
> *as a hen gathers her brood under her wings,*
> *and you were not willing!"*
> MATTHEW 23:37 ESV

Jesus wept when wanting one thing and Jerusalem wanting another. Remarkably, the same Greek word for "wishing, wanting, or willing" (*thelo*) is used for what Jesus wanted and what Jerusalem's people wanted.

Of course Jesus could have overpowered Jerusalem, but sovereignly chose not to. Jesus *will* reign over the New Jerusalem someday, filled with people who love and willingly bow to him. Christ's will shall *ultimately* prevail, even though he permitted it to be *immediately* resisted. Ironically, Jerusalem's rejection of his will was necessary to accomplish the fulfillment of his will through redemption.

> "He is Lord, and those who refuse him as Lord cannot use him as Savior…for to say we receive Christ when in fact we reject his right to reign over us is utter absurdity."
>
> *John MacArthur*

*For our sake he made him to be sin who knew no
sin, so that in him we might become
the righteousness of God.*
2 CORINTHIANS 5:21 ESV

To become sin for us is to become subject on our behalf to the judgment for sin (Romans 6:23). Christ was utterly innocent, yet became damned on our behalf. Not forever, but on the cross as he experienced Hell for us.

The God who is called upon righteously by saints and angels in Heaven to damn people, and called upon habitually by unbelievers flippantly and unrighteously to damn people, in fact damned his Son. He was no victim, but agreed to this from before creation. That he cried out from the cross as one forsaken is unthinkable, and yet it happened...for us.

> "Not all the vials of judgment that have or shall be poured out upon the wicked world give such a demonstration of God's hatred of sin—as the wrath of God let loose upon his Son!"
>
> *Stephen Charnock*

99

*For the joy set before him [Jesus] endured the cross,
scorning its shame, and sat down at the right
hand of the throne of God.*
HEBREWS 12:2

Look again at the remarkable verse above. What was the
joy set before him? The joy of pleasing the Father and
Holy Spirit; redeeming his people; joining with the Spirit
to sanctify his people; granting his people entrance to
Heaven; saying to his people, "Well done" and "Come
and share your master's happiness" (Matthew 25:23); and
seeing his people raised from the dead and watching them
celebrate, never to weep again.

On Good Friday, Jesus experienced the terrible burden of atonement, the trauma of the cross, and the anguish
of being temporarily alienated from his Father when he
became our sin (Matthew 27:46). But this suffering was
overshadowed by the joy of *our* salvation.

> "To bring his chosen [people] to eternal happiness
> was the high ambition which inspired [Jesus Christ],
> and made him wade through a sea of blood."
> *Charles Spurgeon*

"Foxes have holes, and birds of the air have nests, but the Son of Man has nowhere to lay his head."
LUKE 9:58 ESV

Health-and-wealth followers say: "Live like a king's kid." The ultimate "King's kid" was Jesus, but his life looked radically different from royalty.

How did the true "King's kid" live? Born in lowly Bethlehem, raised in despised Nazareth, part of a poor family (compare Leviticus 12:6-8 with Luke 2:22-24). Christ wandered the countryside dependent on others because he didn't have a home. Whatever king's kid the prosperity proponents are speaking of, it obviously isn't Jesus!

Prosperity theology looks at the ascended heavenly Lord rather than the descended earthly servant. Jesus said we must give up everything to be his disciple (Luke 14:33).

In this life, we're to share in his cross—in the next life, we'll share in his crown.

> "There has never been a greater humiliation...than that of Jesus. No one has ever descended so low because no one has ever come from so high."
> *Mark Jones*

Have this mind among yourselves, which is yours in
Christ Jesus, who…emptied himself, by taking the
form of a servant, being born in the likeness of men.
PHILIPPIANS 2:5-7 ESV

Christ is our model of humility. Jesus was called to be a servant and lowered himself. He's given us his footsteps to follow.

Many like to be called a servant, but it's easy to become resentful when we're *treated* like one. Jesus warned his disciples not to follow a lordship model but his servant model (Mark 10:42-45). With Jesus as our example, God also calls us to a lifetime of servanthood, being joyfully used by him to touch others.

When we're used to being served instead of serving others, we can't be Christlike, because he is a servant. May we follow Christ's model of humility and "have this mind among yourselves."

"When Jesus came in the form of a servant, he was not disguising who God is. He was revealing who God is."

John Ortberg

102

> *"The world...hates me because I testify that its works are evil."*
> JOHN 7:7

The world hates Jesus because he tells the truth about our moral condition. Nobody likes being called a sinner! If your goal is to avoid suffering in this life, then following Christ will not help you. Jesus himself said, "If they persecuted me, they will persecute you also" (John 15:20).

But Christ is the King. He calls the shots; we're just his ambassadors. So let's represent the real Jesus, the Jesus of Scripture, not the culturally accommodated "pop Jesus." If we seek our culture's approval, we may get it only at the expense of failing to represent Christ.

> "Plenty of people...have made up a 'Jesus' for themselves, and have found that this invented character makes few real demands on them. He makes them feel happy from time to time, but doesn't challenge them...Which is, of course, what the real Jesus had an uncomfortable habit of doing."
>
> *N.T. Wright*

103

> *"When the Son of Man comes in his glory…he will sit on his glorious throne. All the nations will be gathered before him, and he will separate the people one from another."*
>
> MATTHEW 25:31-32

Christ's words show us there's no middle ground. Either you're a follower of Jesus or you're not.

Jesus referred to Hell as a real place, describing it in graphic terms. He spoke of fire that burns but doesn't consume, an undying worm that eats away at the damned, and a lonely and foreboding darkness (Matthew 10:28; Mark 9:43-48; Matthew 8:12).

Jesus taught that an unbridgeable chasm separates the wicked in Hell from the righteous in Paradise. The wicked suffer terribly, remain conscious, long for relief, and are completely hopeless (Luke 16:19-31). Our Savior painted a bleak picture of Hell.

It isn't just what Jesus said about Hell that matters. It's the fact that it was he who said it.

> "Jesus, the one who rescues us from Hell, is also the one who speaks the most about it."
>
> *Edward Welch*

104

When he said this, all his opponents were humiliated, but the people were delighted with all the wonderful things he was doing.
LUKE 13:17

Can't you imagine folks looking at each other with amazement and nervous glee when Jesus said, "Woe to you, teachers of the law and Pharisees, you hypocrites! You are like whitewashed tombs, which look beautiful on the outside but on the inside are full of the bones of the dead and everything unclean" (Matthew 23:27)?

Jesus was painting mental pictures with a satirical sting. Think of the religious leaders' outrage, compared to the approving smiles of the poor and oppressed, when Jesus said, "The harlots go into the kingdom of God before you" (Matthew 21:31 KJV).

Christ's miracles and words brought much delight wherever he went. The Complete Jewish Bible (CJB) translates Luke 13:17 as "the rest of the crowd were happy about all the wonderful things that were taking place through him."

Outbursts of happiness at Christ's first coming should inspire us to joyfully anticipate his second coming.

> "All life is a festival since the Son of God has redeemed you from death."
>
> *Chrysostom*

> *"I was his daily source of joy,*
> *always happy in his presence—*
> *happy with the world*
> *and pleased with the human race."*
> PROVERBS 8:30-31 GNT

Jesus referred to himself as "wisdom" when he said, "The Son of Man came eating and drinking...But wisdom is proved right by her deeds" (Matthew 11:19).

I agree with many scholars who say Jesus is speaking of himself as the well-known personification of wisdom in Proverbs 8. Wisdom, clearly not just an attribute but a being, says, "I was filled with delight day after day...rejoicing in his whole world and delighting in mankind" (Proverbs 8:30-31).

The Common English Bible (CEB) captures it this way: "I was *having fun, smiling* before him all the time, *frolicking* with his inhabited earth and delighting in the human race" (Proverbs 8:30-31, emphasis added). What an amazing portrayal of the happiness of Jesus!

> "The joy of the Lord is...a playfulness that created and sustains the universe, a laughter that guides history to its glorious end."
>
> *Dylan Demarsico*

106

*"Greater love has no one than this, that someone
lay down his life for his friends."*
JOHN 15:13 ESV

If you know Jesus, then the hand holding yours bears the
calluses of a carpenter who carried a cross for you. When
he opens his hand, you see the gnarled flesh of his nail-
scarred wrists. When you might think he doesn't understand your pain, realize you don't understand the extent
of his.

In *The Reason for God*, Timothy Keller writes, "It can't
be that he is indifferent or detached from our condition.
God takes our misery and suffering *so* seriously that he was
willing to take it on himself."

When you cry out to God, "Why have you let this
happen?" picture the outstretched hands of Christ, forever scarred…for you. Do those look like the hands of a
God who doesn't care?

> "There were no cords could have held him to the
> whipping-post but those of love; no nails have fas-
> tened him to the cross but those of love."
>
> *Thomas Goodwin*

Zacchaeus quickly climbed down and took Jesus to
his house in great excitement and joy.
Luke 19:6 nlt

The Common English Bible says, "Zacchaeus came down at once, *happy* to welcome Jesus" (Luke 19:6). Imagine how this tax collector, despised by Romans for being Jewish and despised by Jews for serving Romans, felt when Jesus invited himself to his home!

The presence of Jesus—his nearness, friendship, and compassion—was the key to all of the disciples' happiness. But he further promises: "I will never leave you or abandon you" (Hebrews 13:5 csb).

We can experience a foretaste now of that future eternal joy. We can rejoice in Jesus as John the Baptist did, when he said, "The friend who attends the bridegroom…is full of joy when he hears the bridegroom's voice. That joy is mine, and it is now complete" (John 3:29).

> "To be in Christ is the source of the Christian's life; to be like Christ is the sum of his excellence; to be with Christ is the fullness of his joy."
>
> *Charles Hodge*

108

*While they were talking…Jesus himself drew near
and went with them…He interpreted to them in
all the Scriptures the things concerning himself.*
LUKE 24:15,27 ESV

The risen Jesus walked and talked with two disciples on
the road to Emmaus. They asked him questions; he taught
them though "they were kept from recognizing him" (v. 16).
Imagine eavesdropping on that conversation!

In difficult times, we also walk the Emmaus road. Sorrow overwhelms us. Questions plague us. We wonder
where God is, when all along he walks beside us.

I look forward to conversations with Jesus where I not
only ask questions but also hear answers from him. One
day we'll be with Jesus and at last understand so much of
what eludes us now.

Until then, God is not silent! He's provided his Word,
his Holy Spirit, and his people to help us understand—
and grace to trust him when we don't.

> "I know now, Lord, why you utter no answer. You are
> yourself the answer."
>
> C.S. Lewis

109

*He also raised us up with him and seated us with
him in the heavens in Christ Jesus.*
EPHESIANS 2:6 CSB

As Christians, we're linked to Heaven in ways too deep to
comprehend. According to Ephesians 2:6, we're somehow
already seated with Christ in Heaven. So we can't be satisfied with less.

Desire is a signpost pointing to Heaven. Every longing
for better health is a longing for perfect bodies we'll have
on the New Earth. Every longing for romance is a longing
for ultimate romance with Christ. Every thirst for beauty
is a thirst for Christ. Every taste of joy is but a foretaste of
more vibrant joy than can presently be found on Earth.

One day we'll realize that as we went down every dead-
end street pursuing what we thought we wanted, it was
really him we were searching for, longing for.

And him alone who could ever satisfy us.

"Created beauty in this world...is a breadcrumb
path that leads us to Christ."

Steve DeWitt

110

"Father, I want those you have given me to be with
me where I am, and to see my glory."
JOHN 17:24

When we accomplish something, we want to share it with those closest to us. Likewise, Jesus wants to share his glory—his person and his accomplishments—with us in Heaven. There's no contradiction between Christ acting for his glory and for our good. The two are synonymous. Our greatest pleasure, our greatest satisfaction, is to behold his glory.

Christ's desire for us to see his glory should touch us deeply. What an unexpected compliment that the Creator of the universe has gone to such great lengths, at such sacrifice, to prepare a place for us where we can behold and participate in his glory.

"Thy main plan, and the end of thy will is to make Christ glorious and beloved in Heaven...In this world thou hast given me a beginning, one day it will be perfected in the realm above."

Puritan Prayer

*For as in Adam all die, so in Christ
all will be made alive.*
1 CORINTHIANS 15:22

God sees the human community as an organic whole; the first Adam represents the fallen race. Likewise, "the last Adam" (1 Corinthians 15:45), King Jesus, represents the new community of God's people. He will undo the damage wrought by the first Adam (1 Corinthians 15:22,45; Romans 5:15-19).

God created Adam and Eve to be king and queen over the Earth, to rule the Earth in righteousness, to the glory of God. They failed. Jesus Christ is the second and last Adam, and the church is his bride, the second Eve. Christ is King, the church his queen. Christ—with his beloved people as his bride and co-rulers—will accomplish on the New Earth what was entrusted to Adam and Eve on the old Earth.

> "The only way sinners can get past the gates of Heaven is by wearing the robes of somebody else's righteousness...the righteousness of Jesus Christ."
>
> *R.C. Sproul*

*"I have brought you glory on earth by finishing
the work you gave me to do."*
JOHN 17:4

What strikes me about these words of Jesus at the end of
his life is not that he worked, or even that he finished his
work, but that the work he finished was what God gave
him to do.

In his book *Crazy Busy*, Kevin DeYoung writes, "*Jesus
didn't do it all.* Jesus didn't meet every need. He left people
waiting in line to be healed. He left one town to preach
to another...And yet, he did everything God asked him
to do."

Jesus knew how to separate the grain of God's will from
the chaff of man's will. This can encourage us to priori-
tize the things in our lives that God has uniquely called
us to do.

> "Whatever you will complete or not today...rest in
> the fact that Jesus has done the most impossible job
> in the world, done it perfectly, and made it avail-
> able. Take it."
>
> *David Murray*

We are therefore Christ's ambassadors,
as though God were making his appeal through us.
We implore you on Christ's behalf:
Be reconciled to God.
2 CORINTHIANS 5:20

Before his ascension, Jesus commanded his disciples to "go and make disciples of all nations" (Matthew 28:19).

Chuck Colson wrote, "The disciples' decision to obey Jesus after the Ascension proved to be a pivot point in history. The world was never the same again."

Everyone we meet has the same need—to know, love, and follow Jesus Christ. He did the hard work of redemption. Our part is to share the good news of great joy with those who desperately need him.

There aren't many joys comparable to leading someone to Christ. It's thrilling and exhilarating. It's also a privilege to sow seeds of good news that may not bear fruit until later. May we daily ask Jesus to give opportunities to share his good news!

"The spirit of Christ is the spirit of missions. The nearer we get to him, the more intensely missionary we become."

Henry Martyn

114

*God shows his love for us in that while we were
still sinners, Christ died for us.*
ROMANS 5:8 ESV

Christ's death on our behalf is sometimes used as a proof of
our worthiness. We were worth dying for, right?

The amazing truth is that Christ died for utterly
unworthy people (Romans 5). Christ's death for us isn't
proof of our value as wonderful people. Rather, it shows
his unfathomable love that he would die for *rotten* people,
wretches like you and me.

The astronomical price of our redemption—the shed
blood of God—is a testimony to how *bad* we really are.
The higher the price, the greater testimony to our deprav-
ity and the wondrous love of God.

It's not only for God's glory but also for our good that
we understand the cross of Christ doesn't show our worth,
but God's.

> "It is not exceptionally worthy people that Jesus loves,
> but his love is exceptional in that he loves those of
> no value at all."
>
> *Jim Elliff*

115

The man who had been demon-possessed begged to go with him. Jesus…said, "Go home to your own people and tell them how much the Lord has done for you, and how he has had mercy on you."

MARK 5:18-19

Jesus loves afflicted people and went to the cross to deliver us, freeing us from evil and suffering. In delivering that desperate demon-possessed man, Jesus gives hope to us all, showing us a picture of the total and final deliverance of his people from the powers of evil.

When Jesus rescued him from evil spirits, the man in Mark 5 was at last "in his right mind," thinking clearly, and he overflowed with gratitude, as should all who know Christ's grace. Embracing Jesus liberates us from considerable evil and suffering, and he calls us to testify to others of his mercy and power.

"No proposition can be more plain than this, that the power of Satan was destroyed by the death of Christ."

John Owen

116

Because he himself suffered when he was tempted,
he is able to help those who are being tempted.
HEBREWS 2:18

Jesus suffered the same trials and temptations we do. God understands our worst losses and heartbreaks, even our temptations.

Dorothy Sayers wrote in *The Whimsical Christian*: "God had the honesty and the courage to take his own medicine…He has himself gone through the whole of human experience, from the trivial irritations of family life and the cramping restrictions of hard work and lack of money to the worst horrors of pain and humiliation, defeat, despair, and death…He was born in poverty and died in disgrace and thought it well worthwhile."

God calls us to hold firmly to our faith precisely because he knows suffering and temptation firsthand.

"The first Adam was tested in the God-blessed garden and fell. The second Adam was tested in the God-cursed desert, and won."

Russell Moore

117

"To the thirsty I will give water without cost from the spring of the water of life."
REVELATION 21:6

Jesus, God's Son, went to the cross to bring us into relationship with God. He is fully worthy of our trust and invites us to come to him to quench our thirst. Christ's absence brings thirst and longing; his presence brings satisfaction.

Jesus quenches our thirst from the inside. The Holy Spirit indwells us so no matter what hostile and heartbreaking circumstances we face, this remains true: "Rivers of living water will flow from within [us]" (John 7:38). Not trickles, not creeks, but full-fledged rivers of life-giving water!

Are you thirsty for happiness—for meaning, peace, contentment? Jesus invites you to join millions throughout history to come to him and drink the best water in the universe—the only refreshment that will ever truly and eternally satisfy.

"Christ is an ever-flowing fountain; he is continually supplying his people, and the fountain is not spent."
Jonathan Edwards

118

Look, he is coming with the clouds,
and every eye will see him.
REVELATION 1:7

When Christ returns, "every eye will see him." How is that physically possible? Will he be in multiple places at one time?

If God took on human form several times, as recorded in Scripture, couldn't Christ choose to take on any form to manifest himself to us? Or might the one body of Jesus be simultaneously present with his people in a million places?

Could we walk with Jesus (not just spiritually, but also physically) while millions of others are also walking with him? Might we be able to touch his hand or embrace him or spend a long afternoon privately conversing with him— not just with his spirit but his whole person?

It may defy our logic, but God is capable of doing far more than we imagine.

> "Wherever we journey, union to Jesus and holiness from his Spirit flowing into us, is our chief and only happiness."
>
> *Robert Murray M'Cheyne*

119

Husbands, love your wives, just as Christ loved the church and gave himself up for her.
EPHESIANS 5:25

One analogy God uses to describe his church is a bride preparing for marriage. To love Christ is to love his bride.

It's trendy for people to say, "I love Jesus, but I hate the church." If you said, "Randy, I want to be your friend. I love you, but hate your wife," I would say, "If you hate Nanci, you can't be my friend. She and I are one. I'm deeply loyal to her. I would die for her." Christ would add, "In fact, I *did* die for her."

We need to fix our eyes on Jesus and be part of the church Christ loves. He sees all the flaws in the church, but he hasn't given up on his bride (Matthew 16:18). Neither should we.

> "I want the whole Christ for my Savior, the whole Bible for my book, the whole church for my fellowship."
>
> *John Wesley*

120

He was oppressed and afflicted,
yet he did not open his mouth;
he was led like a lamb to the slaughter,
and as a sheep before its shearers is silent,
so he did not open his mouth.

Isaiah 53:7

Jesus is the true Shepherd who comes to revive, restore, and give life to the sheep (John 10). But Isaiah 53 relates the Messiah not to a shepherd but to a sheep. It's an amazing and magnificent truth that the Creator, Owner, and Shepherd of the flock became a lowly sheep in order to surrender his life for the other sheep.

When you feel God's silence, look at Christ, the lamb who is silent before the shearers. He shouts to us without opening his mouth: "Don't you see the blood and bruises? Never doubt that I care for you."

"When we think of Christ dying on the cross, we are shown the lengths to which God's love goes in order to win us back to himself."

Sinclair Ferguson

*May the grace of the Lord Jesus Christ,
and the love of God, and the fellowship
of the Holy Spirit be with you all.*
2 Corinthians 13:14

No other religion has an eternally relational Creator God. Some claim that Islam's Allah is simply another name for the God of historic Christianity. But the Quran denies this: "Say not 'Trinity'...For Allah is one Allah: Glory be to Him: (far exalted is He) above having a son."

Allah is a monolithic deity not consisting of Father, Son, and Holy Spirit. In *Delighting in the Trinity*, Michael Reeves poses this question: "How could Allah be loving in eternity? Before he created there was nothing else in existence that he could love...how can a solitary God be eternally and essentially loving when love involves loving another?"

The Trinity beautifully resolves the apparent problem of God's love preexisting any object of his love.

"The Trinity is the cockpit of all Christian thinking."
Michael Reeves

122

*[Christ] was foreknown before the foundation
of the world but was made manifest in
the last times for the sake of you.*
1 PETER 1:20 ESV

Heartbreaking as it was, Adam and Eve's sin did not take God by surprise. Though evil had no part in God's original creation, it was part of his original plan by which he would redeem mankind—and all creation—from sin, corruption, and death. That original plan was decided in eternity past and included Christ's death on the cross to pay the penalty for our sin.

God "chose us in [Christ] *before the creation of the world*" and "*predestined* us for adoption to sonship through Jesus Christ" (Ephesians 1:4-5). This tells us that God didn't devise his redemptive plan all of a sudden after Adam and Eve stumbled.

Christ's crucifixion was God's set purpose, known from eternity past.

> "God's response...from the beginning of time, has been the sacrifice of Jesus Christ on a Roman cross."
> *Matt Chandler*

123

*"And I will put enmity between you and the woman,
and between your offspring and hers."*

GENESIS 3:15

As the culmination of his creation of the universe, God created Adam and Eve. At their fall, evil entered the world. And right then God promised a Redeemer, the woman's offspring.

Thousands of years later, in a fantastic plot twist, God became a humble carpenter, healed the sick, raised the dead, and allowed others to kill him. He rose from the dead, then left, promising to return and live forever with his people.

But suppose you could remove Adam and Eve's sin or Cain and Abel's conflict from history. Remove all wars and heartbreaks, and *you would also take away Jesus,* who would not become one of us, revealing God's character and redeeming us.

The gloomy backdrop of all human suffering, including the crucifixion itself, allows Jesus' grace and mercy to shine with dazzling brightness.

"The gospel, because it is a true story, means all the best stories will be proved...true."

Timothy Keller

124

Salvation is found in no one else, for there is no other name…by which we must be saved.

ACTS 4:12

The gods of Hinduism are many and impersonal; Christianity's God is one and personal. Buddhism offers no forgiveness or divine intervention; Christianity offers both. In Judaism and Islam, people earn status through good works. In Christianity, righteousness is only by Christ's merit. Every other religion is people working their way to God. *Christianity is God working his way to people.*

Jesus became a man and died to offer us eternal life. Jesus asked his Father for another way. There was none. Believing in Jesus is the only way (John 1:12).

The gates of Heaven are open freely to us, but at high cost to Jesus. We don't get any applause for our redemption. God gets it all.

"When you realize just how dependent you are on Jesus for your salvation…you understand why the Bible is so insistent that salvation comes only through faith in him."

Greg Gilbert

*This is the victory that has overcome the world,
even our faith.*
1 JOHN 5:4

None of us are prisoners of natural temperaments. We too quickly underestimate the Holy Spirit's power to transform us gradually into the image of Christ (2 Corinthians 3:18).

Despite human limits, our freedom of will is expanded dramatically when we become united with Christ through faith in him. Jesus said, "If the Son sets you free, you will be free indeed" (John 8:36).

We have a transformed identity—in Christ. We're no longer who we used to be: "The old has gone, the new is here!" (2 Corinthians 5:17). We are Christ's bride, clothed in "fine linen, bright and clean" (Revelation 19:7-8).

So let's not believe that sin is more powerful than Christ. God says otherwise. Scripture tells us to "count yourselves dead to sin but alive to God in Christ Jesus" (Romans 6:11).

"The only way of receiving supplies of spiritual strength and grace from Jesus Christ…is by faith."
John Owen

126

*"This is my beloved Son,
with whom I am well pleased."*
MATTHEW 17:5 ESV

Twice in Matthew's Gospel—at Jesus' baptism and the Transfiguration—we see extraordinary exhibitions of the triune God's happiness.

At Jesus' baptism (Matthew 3:16-17), the Father, Son, and Holy Spirit all participate. The Father audibly expresses pleasure and happiness in the Son, while the Spirit affirms their threefold unity by descending on Jesus like a dove.

At the Transfiguration, the Father's pleasure in his Son is again evidenced (Matthew 17:5). The Father and Son take boundless pleasure in each other, as they do in the Holy Spirit. The Father says, "My servant...in whom I delight" (Isaiah 42:1).

The Father, Son, and Holy Spirit enjoyed one another since before the foundation of the world (John 17:24; 1 Peter 1:20).

> "Before you ever had a happy moment...before the universe was even created—God the Father and God the Son and God the Spirit were enjoying a perfect and robust relational delight in one another."
> *Steve DeWitt*

"You shall love the Lord your God with all your heart… You shall love your neighbor as yourself."
MATTHEW 22:37,39 ESV

Jesus affirmed that the greatest commandment was to love God, and the second, inseparable from the first, was to love our neighbor. One of the highest ways we love God is by loving people.

Jesus rebuked the religious leaders because they imagined they could love God without loving people (Luke 10:25-37). If we don't love people, who are created in God's image, we can't love God (1 John 4:8).

Jesus is our ultimate example of this love. It wasn't a distant love that said, "I love people, what a pity they're going to Hell." It was an authentic love that acted, intervened, and was willing to take the greatest risks and most severe consequences to rescue mankind from destruction.

"I am so flawed that Jesus had to die for me, yet I am so loved and valued that Jesus was glad to die for me."

Timothy Keller

128

Christ Jesus who died—more than that, who was raised to life—is at the right hand of God and is also interceding for us.

ROMANS 8:34

Christ, the God-man, is in Heaven, at the right hand of God, interceding for people on Earth. Since "the prayer of a righteous person is powerful and effective" (James 5:16), what could be more effective than Christ's prayers for us?

Robert Murray M'Cheyne said, "If I could hear Christ praying for me in the next room, I would not fear a million enemies. Yet distance makes no difference. He is praying for me."

Sometimes we sense Christ's presence more than other times. But he is always there helping us and interceding before the Father on our behalf. What an encouragement to know that even if no one knows our needs and is praying for us, Christ does and is!

> "It is a source of joy to the Christian, that the Crucified is now the Glorified...to appear as the High Priest and Intercessor of his people."
>
> *John MacDuff*

*Whoever believes in him is not condemned, but
whoever does not believe stands condemned already.*

JOHN 3:18

God states a reason for his pleasure in his Son: "You have
loved righteousness and hated wickedness" (Hebrews 1:9).
God's attributes of holiness, purity, and righteousness
prompt him to hate evil.

David writes, "The arrogant cannot stand in your presence; you hate all who do wrong" (Psalm 5:5). If we place
God's love above his holiness, such statements will seem
appalling.

The God of love is also a God of wrath (Romans
1:18). The God who punishes is the same loving God who
chose to die in our place to offer us pardon from eternal
punishment.

Any affirmation of God's love that fails to acknowledge
the demands of his holiness distorts God's character and
truth and undermines the gospel.

> "The teaching of Christ on judgment is thus not an
> appendix to the good news…but (strangely per-
> haps) it is part of the very texture of the good news."
> *Paul Helm*

And he took the children in his arms, placed his
hands on them and blessed them.

MARK 10:16

Christ's disciples failed to understand how valuable children were to him and rebuked those who tried to bring them near (Luke 18:15-17). But Jesus said, "Let the little children come to me." He did not consider children a distraction from his Kingdom business, but an integral part of it.

Christ taught that we need to become like children to enter God's Kingdom, and he embraced children when his disciples wanted to exclude them (Matthew 19:13-14). He used children as examples of faith (Matthew 18:2-4). He said the angels assigned to children "continually see the face of My Father who is in heaven" (Matthew 18:10 NASB).

Christ proved his love for children by becoming a child himself, eventually dying for each and every child, showing how precious he considers them to be.

"We...follow the Selfless, Cross-Carrying Servant
of God who welcomed children. May we do the
same."

Kelly Needham

131

Jesus said to them, "Come and have breakfast."
None of the disciples dared ask him, "Who are you?"
They knew it was the Lord.

JOHN 21:12

Jesus spent remarkably normal time with his disciples after his resurrection. One morning, he "stood on the shore" (John 21:4), calling to the disciples (v. 5) with a human voice that didn't sound like the deep, otherworldly voices movies assign to God.

Jesus started a fire and was already cooking fish, which means he didn't just snap his fingers and the finished meal materialized. He invited the disciples to add their fish to his and come have breakfast.

Once we understand Christ's resurrection as the prototype for the resurrection of mankind and the Earth, we realize Scripture has set an interpretive precedent for approaching passages concerning human resurrection and life on the New Earth.

"Peter was made to walk on water in his old body. Imagine what Christ will enable you to do in your new one?"

Larry Dick

132

I saw a Lamb...He went and took the scroll from
the right hand of him who sat on the throne.
REVELATION 5:6-7

Revelation 5 depicts a powerful scene in the present Heaven. God the Father holds a sealed scroll—the Father's will, his plan for the distribution and management of his estate: Earth and its people. But who'll come forward to receive the inheritance?

John writes, "I wept and wept because no one was found who was worthy to open the scroll or look inside" (v. 4). Human sin proved Adam unworthy—and Abraham, David, and every other person in history.

But the story continues: "Do not weep! See, the Lion of the tribe of Judah, the Root of David, has triumphed. He is able to open the scroll and its seven seals" (v. 5).

We have one reason not to weep: Jesus and his utter worthiness to redeem us!

> "All of salvation is from and about Jesus. No one can boast. He starts and finishes it."
>
> *Trillia Newbell*

133

"Woe to you teachers of the law and Pharisees, you hypocrites! You are like whitewashed tombs, which look beautiful on the outside but on the inside are full of...everything unclean."

MATTHEW 23:27

Some people think being Christlike means we should never lovingly confront others or do anything unpopular. By those standards, Jesus wasn't Christlike. Remember how he confronted the money changers, called them hypocrites, and chased them out of the temple?

Jesus shows us exactly what God looks like. Problems arise when we trust our own subjective picture of Jesus. Sometimes we believe in a Jesus of our imaginations, who is more like Mr. Rogers or Barney the Dinosaur than the powerful and controversial Jesus of Scripture.

We're not God's speechwriters. We are to deliver his message, not compose it. He's already done that—it's called the Bible.

"God is compassionate and just, loving and holy, wrathful and forgiving. We can't sideline his more difficult attributes to make room for the palatable ones."

Francis Chan

134

*"I will make…the ends of the earth your possession.
You shall break them with a rod of iron
and dash them in pieces like a potter's vessel."*
PSALM 2:8-9 ESV

Psalm 2 speaks of Christ ruling "with a rod of iron" and dashing the nations to pieces "like pottery," a reference to the Messiah's return and judgment. But once we enter the New Heavens and New Earth, there's no iron rule or dashing to pieces, for there's no more rebellion, sin, or death. The vanquishing of sin means only the end of Christ's *contested* rule and the beginning of his eternal rule.

In God's unaltered plan for the New Earth, nations still exist and kings come into the New Jerusalem bringing tribute to the King of kings (Revelation 21:24,26).

"Through his resurrection and ascension the King has been enthroned. The universe is his…His authority is absolute and exhaustive. You will never breathe air that doesn't belong to him and you will suffocate if you try."

Sam Allberry

135

For in him all things were created...
and in him all things hold together.
COLOSSIANS 1:16-17

We often hear about messages from the spirit realm, supposedly from people who've died and returned from Heaven to visit loved ones. Yet they rarely express wonder at seeing Jesus.

But no one who'd actually experienced Heaven would neglect mentioning Scripture's main focus. After an evening dining with a king, you wouldn't return talking about place settings. When John wrote about what he was shown in Heaven, he recorded details—but never stopped talking about Jesus.

Christ "upholds the universe by the word of his power" (Hebrews 1:3 ESV). The Greek word translated "upholds" is *phero,* "to carry," the same word used in Luke 5:18 when the paralyzed man was carried on his mat to Jesus. God carries the entire universe as men carry a bed.

> "When we weigh who Christ is and what he has done, not only are we enriched, but he is glorified as well."
>
> *Joni Eareckson Tada*

136

*"Look at the birds of the air…Are you not much
more valuable than they?"*

MATTHEW 6:26

Jesus says God cares for the birds. Yet birds aren't created
in God's image. Christ didn't die for birds. The Holy Spirit
doesn't indwell birds. Birds won't reign with Christ. But
we will! So Christ asks his disciples, "Are you not much
more valuable than they?"

In Matthew 6:33, Jesus says, "Seek first his kingdom
and his righteousness, and all these things [what you eat,
drink, and wear] will be given to you as well." Unlike the
pagans who "run after all these things" and "worry about
tomorrow," believers are told to follow Christ, live a radical life of faith, and trust God to provide.

If he takes care of the less valuable creatures, he will certainly take care of us!

"We have no cause of fear. His eye is upon us, his
arm over us, his ear open to our prayer—his grace
sufficient, his promise unchangeable."

John Newton

137

Whoever believes in the Son of God accepts this testimony. Whoever does not believe God has made him out to be a liar.

1 John 5:10

As unbelievers we "were dead in the trespasses and sins in which [we] once walked" (Ephesians 2:1-2 ESV). God's standard is perfection (Matthew 5:48). The God who requires moral perfection is the God who supplies it in Jesus.

We need not be sinlessly perfect to please God, but we *must* believe that Christ's murder was *done by us* before we can understand that God *intended it for us*, achieving our moral perfection that's required to live forever with God. Only then can we be transformed into righteous beings who please God (2 Corinthians 5:21).

Had Christ not gone to the cross, we would have borne the judgment for our sins. But since he did, the greatest sin is choosing not to trust him for his redemptive work.

"We are secure, not because we hold tightly to Jesus, but because he holds tightly to us."

R.C. Sproul

138

*Carrying his own cross he went out to the place of
the Skull (which in Aramaic is called Golgotha).
There they crucified him.*

JOHN 19:17-18

What is good about Good Friday, the day Christ was crucified? Why isn't it called Bad Friday? Because *we see it in
retrospect*. From the appallingly bad came the inexpressibly
good. Therefore, we don't call it Pointless Friday or Horrible Friday. Instead, we call it *Good* Friday. The eternal good
of that dreadful day eclipses even the temporary evil of the
great suffering of God's Son.

On the cross Jesus suffered the worst pain in history.
Yet that event will forever remain at the center of our worship and wonder. If God used the most terrible event in
history for eternal good, surely he will use the most terrible events in our lives for eternal good.

> "The cross stands as a reminder that God, in grace,
> takes very bad things and turns them into very good
> things."
>
> *Paul David Tripp*

For the message of the cross is foolishness to those who are perishing, but to us who are being saved it is the power of God.
1 CORINTHIANS 1:18

The problem of reconciling evil people with an evil-hating God is history's greatest problem. It calls for the greatest solution ever devised, one so radical as to be unthinkable, offending innumerable sensibilities: the cross of Jesus.

If redemption could've been purchased at a lower cost, surely God would've done so. But God cannot exercise one attribute in disregard of others. Therefore, the omnipotent God couldn't save us while leaving his holiness unsatisfied.

Everything before the cross points forward to it. Everything since the cross points back to it. Everything that will last was purchased on it. Everything that matters hinges on it.

"Love was compressed for all history in that lonely figure on the cross, who said that he could call down angels at any moment on a rescue mission, but chose not to—because of us."

Philip Yancey

*When they hurled their insults at him, he did not
retaliate; when he suffered, he made no threats.*
1 Peter 2:23

Jesus felt overwhelming sadness in the garden of Gethsemane. Then the soldiers mocked and struck him. And after their brutality, Jesus went to the cross to die for us.

Why did Jesus hang on the cross for six hours rather than six seconds or six minutes? Perhaps as a reminder that suffering is a process. God doesn't always end our suffering as soon as we'd like. We're in good company with Jesus.

One look at Jesus silences the argument that God maintains his distance from human suffering. God doesn't merely empathize with sufferings. He actually suffers.

He paid the highest price on our behalf. God's love for us is soaked in divine blood.

"Jesus lost all his glory so that we could be clothed in it. He was shut out so we could get access. He was bound, nailed, so that we could be free."

Timothy Keller

141

And having disarmed the powers and authorities,
he made a public spectacle of them, triumphing
over them by the cross.

COLOSSIANS 2:15

We're accustomed to sports competitions in which either side can lose. God and Satan are currently at war, but unlike human competitions, they are not equals, and there's no possibility God will lose. Because of the cross, Christ's victory over Satan and death wasn't just possible; it's absolutely certain.

Satan and Jesus don't engage in hand-to-hand combat, with Satan sometimes getting the edge. That's not the Bible; that's Star Wars. Many of us make Satan too big and God too small. Yet the battle is real and not without cost.

But Scripture always describes Satan's power in the context of God's absolute sovereignty. Satan remains under Christ's authority at all times. The devil is nowhere close to being omnipotent, omniscient, omnipresent, or anything like God.

> "The weapon with which Christ warred against the devil, and obtained a most complete victory...was the cross."
>
> *Jonathan Edwards*

142

Jesus said, "It is finished." With that, he
bowed his head and gave up his spirit.
JOHN 19:30

When Jesus said, "It is finished," he used the Greek word *teleo*, which was commonly written over certificates of debt that were fully paid. It means "nothing more is owed." Jesus died so our certificate of debt, listing all our sins, could be marked "paid in full."

Christ didn't take on 99.9 percent of our sin and guilt, and we must carry the remaining 0.1 percent. He took on *all* of it. A friend told me he'd failed God so many times he no longer felt worthy of God's grace. But he was never worthy in the first place! Neither am I. Only Christ is worthy.

Jesus suffered for our sins so we wouldn't have to. When we refuse to joyfully accept what he's already done, we imply that he died in vain.

"Jesus' last word is our first word. It is finished. When he died, our life began."

Louie Giglio

*"Is a lamp brought in to be put under a basket,
or under a bed, and not on a stand?"*
MARK 4:21 ESV

In Jesus' day lamps had open flames, and a bed wasn't a metal frame but a straw mattress. This absurd imagery becomes humorous. (Given his incredible wit along with his loving heart, people must have thought, *What's he going to say next?*)

Jesus said, "It is not the healthy who need a doctor, but the sick. I have not come to call the righteous, but sinners" (Mark 2:17). Imagine healthy people lined up to see a doctor—how laughable!

His humor is far more apparent when we understand his culture and engaging personality. There's nothing disrespectful about noticing that many of Jesus' statements are, by design, happily outrageous. We enjoy laughter because Jesus did, and we are made in his image.

"Once we realize that Christ was not always engaged in pious talk, we have made an enormous step on the road to understanding."

Elton Trueblood

144

Jesus answered [Pilate], "You would have no power over me if it were not given to you from above."
JOHN 19:11

Pilate was the most powerful person in Jerusalem. He wanted Jesus to acknowledge this, asking him, "Do you not know that I have authority to release you and authority to crucify you?" (John 19:10 ESV). Unimpressed, Jesus answered him, "You would have no authority over me at all unless it had been given you from above" (19:11 ESV).

God is not the author of evil. Neither is he ever its victim. His hands are never tied by evil. When Jesus went to the cross he didn't fall into Satan's trap—Satan fell into his. Wills were being exercised, but men didn't call the shots. God did.

Let it never be said that Jesus of Nazareth was a victim of circumstances.

"The victim was the victor, and the cross is still the throne from which he rules the world."

John Stott

145

*"The glory that you have given me I have given to
them...I in them and you in me, that they may
become perfectly one."*
JOHN 17:22,23 ESV

As a young believer, I often heard testimonies of people
happily recalling the day the gospel took hold of their
hearts. But besides happiness about what Jesus did in the
past (on the cross and at my conversion) and what he'll do
in the future (at his return), I should also be happy in what
he's doing today.

Consider that God's Spirit indwells believers (1 Corinthians 6:19). Jesus, too, indwells us (Colossians 1:27). What
about the Father? Jesus' prayer to the Father, "I in them and
you in me," suggests the Father's presence indwells us too.

So within us we have the triune God and his eternally
joyous interrelationship. This is an astounding reality that
should infuse our lives with wonder and delight!

"There is every element of joy—deep, ecstatic, satis-
fying, sanctifying joy—in the gospel of Christ."
Octavius Winslow

146

"You will recognize them by their fruits. Are grapes gathered from thornbushes, or figs from thistles?"
MATTHEW 7:16 ESV

Throughout the Gospels, Jesus made many serious points in humorous ways. People who worked the ground in that culture surely smiled at the self-evident answers about grapes and figs.

Jewish humor frequently employed witty hyperbole—clever, over-the-top statements. But Christ never ridiculed the weak-minded or unfortunate. He did, however, amusingly call out hypocrites in powerful positions.

Jesus said, "When you give to the needy, sound no trumpet before you, as the hypocrites do" (Matthew 6:2 ESV). They wouldn't so obviously promote themselves, but walking slowly and piously, they'd make their money clearly visible.

Jesus called these self-congratulatory actions "sounding a trumpet," undoubtedly producing numerous smiles in the onlookers and menacing stares from the professional hypocrites. And yet, he willingly died for them too!

> "Jesus'…blistering diatribe against the religious leaders of Jerusalem in Matthew 23 ends with Christ weeping over Jerusalem. Compassion colored everything he did."
>
> *John MacArthur*

But we preach Christ crucified...Christ the power
of God and the wisdom of God.
1 Corinthians 1:23-24

A photograph hangs in my office of primitive tribal people watching a movie portrayal of Jesus' crucifixion. The abject shock and horror on their faces and tears in their eyes remind me daily of what it's like to see the cross through fresh eyes.

I've seen people watching the *Jesus* film in their own languages, viewing Jesus with awe, then crying out in agony when he is tortured. They gasp and stare wide-eyed at Christ being nailed to the cross. It's a stunning sight.

Why do we often no longer respond to Jesus' sacrifice that way? Because the good news has become old news. When the gospel story fails to amaze us, we should ask God for a renewed awareness of Jesus' suffering and love.

"We have grown so accustomed to the idea of divine love...that we no longer sense the awe that God's coming should awaken in us."

Dietrich Bonhoeffer

148

> *"I lay down my life that I may take it up again.*
> *No one takes it from me, but I lay it down*
> *of my own accord."*
> JOHN 10:17-18 ESV

Much is learned about Jesus from C.S. Lewis's character Aslan in *The Lion, the Witch, and the Wardrobe*. Knowing he could kill his mocking enemies with one word, instead Aslan allows himself to be bound on the stone table, dying for Edmund, who betrayed him.

Though he could have called down 72,000 angels to defend himself, Jesus chose suffering (Matthew 26:53). With our redemption in view, he endured humiliating torture and execution.

With one word, Christ could have called upon those angelic warriors to bring him instant relief. But instead he showed incredible restraint and single-minded purpose in purchasing our eternal salvation.

Perhaps the greatest wonder is not that Jesus went to the cross but that he *stayed* on it.

> "It is at the cross that we see God most clearly. If history were the vastness of space, the cross would be its brightest star."
>
> *Chris Tomlinson*

At noon, darkness came over the whole land…
And at three in the afternoon Jesus cried out in a
loud voice, "Eloi, Eloi, lema sabachthani?"
(which means "My God, my God,
why have you forsaken me?").
MARK 15:33-34

In that haunting cry on the cross, Jesus identified with our despair and bridged the gap between God and us not only theologically but emotionally—between our agonizing cries and those of God's Son.

The beloved Son who had "well pleased" his Father (Matthew 3:17) became our sin (2 Corinthians 5:21). So the Father turned away. For the first time in all eternity, the oneness within the Godhead knew separation. In ways we cannot comprehend—ways that would amount to blasphemy had not God revealed it to us—the atonement somehow tore God apart.

"Let a man once see his God down in the arena as a Man—suffering, tempted, sweating, and agonized, finally dying a criminal's death—and he is a hard man indeed who is untouched."

J.B. Phillips

150

"Now my soul is troubled, and what shall I say?
'Father, save me from this hour'? No, it was for this
very reason I came to this hour."
JOHN 12:27-28

Some believe that Jesus' cry, "My God, my God, why have you forsaken me?" (Matthew 27:46) showed he didn't know why the Father's wrath poured out on him. But Scripture says otherwise. Jesus knew why he had to die. He cried out because any separation from his Father constituted an infinite horror.

Saying, "It is finished" (John 19:30), the redemptive price having been paid, Jesus ceased to bear the penalty for our sin. Then he called out, "Father, into your hands I commit my spirit" (Luke 23:46).

The unimaginable had happened. Once redemption was accomplished in space-time history, the triune God was restored to the complete oneness known from eternity past and assured for eternity future.

> "At the cross...Jesus, God's beloved Son, takes the retributive punishment that we deserved, even separation from God, to deliver us."
>
> *Robert Peterson*

151

But he was pierced for our transgressions,
he was crushed for our iniquities...
and by his wounds we are healed.

Isaiah 53:5

If I had to believe that this world is God's best, I wouldn't be a Christian. No matter how persuasive the argument, I couldn't overcome the obstacles of suffering children or slaughters like the Holocaust.

If it weren't for Jesus—if God had not become a man and given himself for the sins of the world, if he hadn't taken upon himself greater suffering and evil than anyone else ever—I wouldn't have faith in God. The fault would lie with me, for God would still be good, but I wouldn't *know* that.

Because of what Jesus has done, I can look at him and say, "Yes, Lord, I will trust you. You've proven yourself."

"Christ was...wounded that I might be healed... tormented that I might be comforted, made a shame that I might inherit glory, entered darkness that I might have eternal light."

Puritan Prayer

*Against its will, all creation was subjected to God's curse.
But with eager hope, the creation looks forward
to the day when it will join God's children
in glorious freedom from death and decay.*
ROMANS 8:20-21 NLT

The power of Christ's resurrection is enough not only to remake us, but also the universe. Isaac Watts' hymn "Joy to the World" is theologically on target:

> No more let sins and sorrows grow
> Nor thorns infest the ground;
> He comes to make His blessings flow
> Far as the curse is found.

How far does Christ's redemptive work extend? *Far as the curse is found.* If redemption failed to reach the farthest boundaries of the curse, it would be incomplete. God won't be satisfied until every sin, sorrow, and thorn is reckoned with.

Let's rejoice as we anticipate the height, depth, length, and breadth of our Savior's redemptive work!

"In God's mighty act of raising Jesus bodily from the grave, we're right to glimpse the final chapter of redemption's drama."

M.D. Williams

*This is love: not that we loved God,
but that he loved us and sent his Son
as an atoning sacrifice for our sins.*
1 JOHN 4:10

A powerful moment in the movie *The Passion of the Christ* occurs when Jesus is lying on the ground as guards kick, mock, and spit on him. A horrified woman pleads, "Someone, stop this!"

The great irony is that had someone delivered Jesus from his suffering, he couldn't have delivered us from ours.

If we'd witnessed firsthand Gethsemane and the march to Golgotha and the horrific cross, we'd never question God's empathy or love. He recorded those events in his Word so we might see them in our mind's eye; if we do, our preoccupation with injustices done against us will diminish.

God understands what it means to be utterly abandoned, suffer terribly, and die miserably.

"Calvary is the supreme demonstration of Divine love. Whenever you are tempted to doubt the love of God…go back to Calvary."

A.W. Pink

154

> *"The kingdom of God is not coming in ways*
> *that can be observed...the kingdom of God*
> *is in the midst of you."*
> LUKE 17:20-21 ESV

Jesus said, "My kingdom is not of this world. If it were, my servants would fight to prevent my arrest by the Jewish leaders" (John 18:36).

When Jesus said this, he didn't mean his Kingdom wouldn't be *on* this Earth after it's transformed. He meant it isn't *of* this Earth as it is now, under the curse. Although Christ's Kingdom isn't *from* the Earth, it extends *to* the Earth, and one day will be centered *on* the Earth. Christ's Kingdom touches this world now through his indwelling Spirit, the presence of the church, and his providential reign.

> "Whenever Christ is enthroned as King, the Kingdom of God is come...While we cannot say that he is ruling over all in the world at the present time, he is certainly ruling in that way in the hearts and lives of all his people."
>
> *Martyn Lloyd-Jones*

155

Then the King will say… "Come, you who are blessed by my Father, inherit the kingdom prepared for you from the foundation of the world."

MATTHEW 25:34 ESV

God's plan culminates after the final judgment, when King Jesus says to his people, "Take your inheritance, the kingdom prepared for you." Where is this Kingdom? Exactly where it's been all along—on Earth.

What's the inheritance Jesus speaks of? Just as children of kings inherit kingdoms, and kingdoms consist of land and property, so Earth is humanity's God-given property.

Christ is saying, "This is what I wanted for you. This is what I went to the cross and defeated death to give you. Take it, rule it, enjoy it; and share my happiness."

"Can you imagine living in a society where everyone is so happy with leadership decisions?…Can you imagine a world where no one ever again complains about government? Yes, it's possible! It's predicted. It's prepared. It's the Kingdom of heaven. And it's real!"

Larry Dick

156

*Since, then, you have been raised with Christ, set
your hearts on things above, where Christ is,
seated at the right hand of God.*

Colossians 3:1

Many people have told me, "We shouldn't think about
Heaven. We should just think about Jesus." But this view-
point is clearly contradicted by Scripture.

Colossians 3 is a direct command to set our hearts and
minds on Heaven. We do this because we love Jesus, and
Heaven is where he now resides. To long for Heaven is to
long for Christ. To long for Christ is to long for Heaven.

> "Christ did not die to forgive sinners who go on trea-
> suring anything above seeing and savoring God.
> And people who would be happy in Heaven if
> Christ were not there, will not be there. The gos-
> pel is not a way to get people to Heaven; it is a
> way to get people to God...If we don't want God
> above all things, we have not been converted by
> the gospel."
>
> *John Piper*

157

Christ also suffered once for sins, the righteous for
the unrighteous, that he might bring us to God.
1 PETER 3:18 ESV

No tragedy is greater than God's blameless Son being slaughtered in horrid crucifixion. Yet as a result, countless people will spend eternity with God in joyful celebration and endless pleasure. Jesus himself will be forever exalted, and all will recognize him as Lord, to the glory of God the Father. Eternal benefits are ours, all because he suffered.

Though many recent writers have spoken of God's vulnerability and weakness demonstrated on the cross, we must see this truth in the context of God's sovereignty. The obedient death of Jesus on the cross reflects a deliberate weakness. He willingly chose to suffer as a victim.

Scripture portrays a God so strong that he can take on weakness to overpower opposition and accomplish his eternal purposes.

> "No power in this world, however powerful, acts outside of the sovereign reign and plan of a God who died for us."
>
> *Marshall Segal*

158

You will receive a rich welcome into the eternal kingdom of our Lord and Savior Jesus Christ.
2 PETER 1:11

To meet an earthly king would be the ultimate experience. How much greater will it be to see King Jesus in his glory? There's no higher privilege, no greater thrill.

I imagine myself seeing Jesus, falling to my knees, having him reach out and pull me up. To think of him welcoming me not just once, but for all eternity, is sheer joy.

Together, we'll rejoice crying, "You are worthy, our Lord and God, to receive glory and honor and power" (Revelation 4:11). What could be greater than worshiping him, hearing him say, "Well done, my good and faithful servant," and enjoying our Master's happiness? (Matthew 25:21).

> "All that puzzles us now will become plain to us in the light of the Lamb...Oh! what a manifestation!... to be present and to see him in his own light, the King of kings, and Lord of lords!"
>
> *Charles Spurgeon*

159

Holy, holy, holy is the LORD Almighty…
God is love.
ISAIAH 6:3; 1 JOHN 4:8

Christ reveals God's love *and* holiness. Citing Isaiah 6:10, John then adds, "Isaiah…saw Jesus' glory" (John 12:41). When? When he beheld God and heard seraphim emphasize his holiness, crying out three times "holy, holy, holy" (Isaiah 6:3). We can't choose God's love over holiness, or holiness over love.

If God's love outstripped his holiness, then why send Jesus to the cross? If love trumps holiness, then why not dispense with the crucifixion altogether? God's holiness and love combined at Calvary constitute the only way to save sinners and still satisfy God's perfect nature.

God's love divorced from the full picture of his infinite glory reduces him to a false god, made in our likeness. God's love, defined in light of the totality of his all-encompassing majesty, depicts him as he is and invites our heartfelt praise.

> "Jesus is holiness with a face. To be holy is to be like him."
>
> *Nancy DeMoss Wolgemuth*

160

"The kingdom of the world has become the kingdom of our Lord and of his Christ, and he will reign for ever and ever."

REVELATION 11:15 ESV

Scripture says that on the New Earth, where Christ will reign, there will be nations with their own leaders. Just as the "wise men," kings of foreign nations, once came to worship the newborn Christ, so on the New Earth "wise men" will journey to the New Jerusalem: "The nations will walk by its light, and the kings of the earth will bring their splendor into it…The glory and honor of the nations will be brought into it" (Revelation 21:24,26).

We'll humbly bow before King Jesus, joyfully worshiping him seated on the throne. We'll offer him treasures from our nations, and he'll be pleased to receive them. The King will gladly entrust the ruling of these nations to those who served him faithfully in this life.

"Whosoever will reign with Christ in Heaven, must have Christ reigning in him on Earth."

John Wesley

And the Word became flesh and dwelt among us,
and we have seen his glory, glory as of the only Son
from the Father, full of grace and truth.
JOHN 1:14 ESV

When Jesus stepped onto the world's stage, people not only heard the demands of truth but saw Truth himself. No longer fleeting glimmers of grace, but Grace himself.

Passing in front of Moses, God identified himself as "abounding in love and faithfulness" (Exodus 34:6). The words translated *love* and *faithfulness* are the Hebrew equivalents of *grace* and *truth*.

Christ's hearers had seen truth in the Law of Moses, but it was Christ who personified grace. The law could only reveal sin. Jesus could *remove* it.

We need Christians who, like Jesus, are full of grace and truth. People with both sound doctrine and warm hearts, reaching out to all the needy in the name of Christ.

> "Jesus did not come to strike a balance between grace and truth. He brought the full measure of both."
>
> *Andy Stanley*

Since [God's] children have flesh and blood, [Jesus] too shared in their humanity so that by his death he might destroy him who holds the power of death— that is, the devil—and free those who all their lives were held in slavery by their fear of death.

HEBREWS 2:14-15

Scripture portrays God as holy and transcendent. But even before Christ's incarnation, God came to the garden to walk with Adam and Eve. And Christ's incarnation and resurrection took it much further—one member of the transcendent triune God became permanently immanent. Jesus is in physical form, in a human resurrection body, for all eternity.

He may choose to exercise his divine omnipresence in a way we can't comprehend, but Jesus the risen Savior will not cease to be the eternal God-man.

"Christ is the humility of God embodied in human nature; the Eternal Love humbling itself, clothing itself in the garb of meekness and gentleness, to win and serve and save us."

Andrew Murray

163

*"Truly, I say to you, only with difficulty will a rich
person enter the kingdom of heaven."*
MATTHEW 19:23 ESV

Christ said, "It is easier for a camel to go through the eye
of a needle than for someone who is rich to enter the kingdom of God" (Matthew 19:24). Hearing this, the disciples
were astonished, asking, "Who then can be saved?" (19:25).

Why the astonishment? Because they thought wealth
was a sign of God's approval. They hadn't yet grasped the
significance of Jesus' lifestyle. Jesus, whose Father was "well
pleased" with him (Matthew 3:17), lived in poverty, had
no place to lay his head (Matthew 8:20), and owned only
a robe and sandals.

After all, if wealth is a sign of God's approval and poverty shows his disapproval, then Jesus and Paul were on
God's blacklist, and drug dealers and embezzlers are the
apple of his eye.

"Prosperity is a great mercy, but adversity is a greater
one, if it brings us to Christ."

J.C. Ryle

164

*"'Love the Lord your God with all your heart
and with all your soul and with all your
strength and with all your mind'; and,
'Love your neighbor as yourself.'"*
LUKE 10:27

An expert in the law asked Jesus, "And who is my neighbor?" (Luke 10:29). He was seeking a narrow definition of the word *neighbor* to avoid responsibility for others.

Jesus then told a story. A man was beaten and left half dead. A priest and a Levite passed by him. But a despised Samaritan exercised the law of love by caring for him.

Jesus asked the expert which man acted as a neighbor. He replied, "The one who had mercy on him." And Jesus said, "Go and do likewise" (Luke 10:37).

The message is clear: Jesus came to serve the whole world, and every person was his neighbor, and should be ours.

"The mark of Christian discipleship is love...the kind that Jesus exercised toward his followers, love visible enough that men will recognize it as belonging to those people who follow Jesus."

Thabiti Anyabwile

*If Christ has not been raised, your faith is futile; you
are still in your sins. Then those also who have fallen
asleep in Christ are lost. If only for this life we have
hope in Christ, we are of all people most to be pitied.*
1 CORINTHIANS 15:17-19

The physical resurrection of Jesus is the cornerstone of
redemption. Without it and what it means—an eternal future for fully restored humans dwelling on a fully
restored Earth—there's no Christianity.

Paul considered the resurrection essential to the Christian faith. He said if Christ didn't rise from the dead, we're
still in our sins—meaning we're bound for Hell, not
Heaven.

> "How different is the epitaph on the tomb of Jesus! It
> is neither written in gold nor cut in stone. It is spoken
> by the mouth of an angel and is the exact reverse of
> what is put on all other tombs: 'He is not here; for
> he is risen' (Matthew 28:6)."
>
> *Billy Graham*

166

*"No longer will they teach their neighbor,
or say to one another, 'Know the Lord,'
because they will all know me."*

JEREMIAH 31:34

There will always be more to see when we look at Jesus, because his infinite character can never be exhausted. We could—and will—spend countless millennia exploring the depths of God's being. This is the magnificence of God and the wonder of Heaven.

We'll spend eternity worshiping, exploring, and serving Christ, seeing his magnificent beauty in everything and everyone around us. In the new universe, as we study nature and pursue science and mathematics and every realm of knowledge, we'll see him in everything, for he's behind it all.

And yet, all our explorations and adventures and projects in Heaven will pale in comparison to the wonder of seeing Jesus face-to-face.

"Without Christ, life is as the twilight with dark night ahead; with Christ, it is the dawn of morning with the light and warmth of a full day ahead."

Philip Schaff

*"They also will answer, 'Lord, when did we see you
hungry or thirsty or a stranger or needing clothes
or sick or in prison, and did not help you?' He will
reply, 'Truly I tell you, whatever you did not do for
one of the least of these, you did not do for me.'"*
MATTHEW 25:44-45

Many imagine that though God once suffered on the cross,
he's now remote and distant from suffering. Not so! After
his ascension, Jesus said, "Saul, Saul, why do you persecute me?" (Acts 9:4).

Jesus made it clear that to persecute his people is to persecute him. Christ no longer suffers on the cross, but he
suffers with his people.

It's certain that each of us will suffer in this life. But
we're not alone. Jesus suffered for us, he suffers with us,
and many throughout the world suffer alongside us as we
follow our suffering Savior.

"Christ leads me through no darker rooms than he
went through before."

Richard Baxter

168

"And we bring you the good news that what God promised to the fathers, this he has fulfilled to us their children by raising Jesus."
ACTS 13:32-33 ESV

God sent Jesus at the perfect time for Israel. The hand of Rome was heavy on the Jewish people, and life under an emperor who claimed to be god was particularly oppressive.

The people were equally burdened by stern requirements placed on them by religious leaders. Many Pharisees were obsessed with the law and emphasized self-righteous works over God's grace.

This was the weary and hopeless world into which God brought "good news that will cause great joy" (Luke 2:10). The holy and happy God came to Earth to deliver us from eternal sin and misery.

This world is cursed with sin and suffering, but these obstacles can't trump joy. Christ has come, and with him came light, hope, and redemption—the down payment of this world's final transformation.

"Heaven enters wherever Christ enters, even in this life."

C.S. Lewis

169

*So they departed quickly from the tomb with fear
and great joy, and ran to tell his disciples.*
MATTHEW 28:8 ESV

Seeing the risen Jesus was the ultimate happiness for the
disciples (John 20:20). Similarly, the women at the tomb
responded to the resurrection with great happiness.

You would think their joy wouldn't last, but it contin-
ued after Jesus ascended: "He left them and was taken up
into heaven. Then they worshiped him and returned to
Jerusalem with great joy" (Luke 24:51-52).

Because Jesus was alive, and he promised to be with
them always and return one day, their joy ran deep and
overflowed the banks of their lives. The same can be true
for us.

> "A person who is in real communion with God...is
> happy. It does not matter whether he is in a dun-
> geon, or whether he has his feet fast in the stocks, or
> whether he is burning at the stake; he is still happy
> if he is in communion with God."
>
> *Martyn Lloyd-Jones*

> *But our citizenship is in heaven. And we eagerly*
> *await a Savior from there, the Lord Jesus Christ, who,*
> *by the power that enables him to bring everything*
> *under his control, will transform our lowly bodies so*
> *that they will be like his glorious body.*
> PHILIPPIANS 3:20-21

Christ's resurrected body, before his ascension, was quite normal in appearance. But what's his "glorious body" like? We're given a picture on the Mount of Transfiguration: "There he was transfigured before them. His face shone like the sun, and his clothes became as white as the light" (Matthew 17:2).

When John was taken into Heaven and saw Jesus there, he fell on his face. He saw the divine glory of the God-man. Coming from a sinful world, his entrance into Heaven and the sight of his risen Savior overwhelmed him (Revelation 1:17-18). The Carpenter from Nazareth was, and will ever be, the King of kings.

> "The work of God in the cross of Christ strikes us as awe-inspiring only after we have first been awed by the glory of God."
>
> *Matt Chandler*

*"The Son of Man is about to be delivered into the
hands of men, and they will kill him, and he will
be raised on the third day."*
MATTHEW 17:22-23 ESV

In the 1990s, scholars gathered to evaluate whether
Jesus' words in the Gospels were actually said. Employ-
ing remarkably subjective criteria, members of the "Jesus
Seminar" were still widely quoted as Christian authorities.

Marcus Borg, a Jesus Seminar leader, said: "For me, it
is irrelevant whether or not the tomb was empty. Whether
Easter involved something remarkable happening to the
physical body of Jesus is irrelevant." He couldn't be more
wrong.

Christianity rises or falls on the resurrection. If this
event is historically true, it makes all other religions false,
because Jesus claimed to be the only way to God. To prove
this, he predicted he would rise three days after his death.
And he did.

"Outside of the cross of Jesus Christ, there is no hope
in this world. That cross and resurrection at the core
of the gospel is the only hope for humanity."
Ravi Zacharias

"And do not fear those who kill the body but cannot kill the soul. Rather fear him who can destroy both soul and body in hell."

MATTHEW 10:28 ESV

We may pride ourselves in thinking we're too loving to believe in Hell. But in saying this, we blaspheme, for we claim to be more loving than Jesus—more loving than the One who with outrageous love took upon himself the penalty for our sin.

Who are we to think we are better than Jesus? Or that when it comes to Hell, or anything else, we know better than he does?

By denying Hell's reality, we lower redemption's stakes and minimize Christ's work on the cross. If he didn't deliver us from a real and eternal Hell, then his work on the cross is less heroic, less potent, less consequential, and less deserving of our worship and praise.

> "It is impossible to be a follower of Christ while denying, disregarding, discrediting, and disbelieving the words of Christ."
>
> *David Platt*

> *"Blessed are you when people hate you, when*
> *they exclude you and insult you...Rejoice in*
> *that day and leap for joy, because great is*
> *your reward in heaven."*
> LUKE 6:22-23

The apostles didn't enjoy suffering, but rejoiced in the midst of it, trusting God's sovereign plan and looking forward to Christ's return, their bodily resurrection, and the redemption of all creation.

Our optimism isn't in the prosperity gospel, which claims God will spare us of suffering. Peter said, "Rejoice inasmuch as you participate in the sufferings of Christ, so that you may be overjoyed when his glory is revealed" (1 Peter 4:13). Christ's future glory is the reason for our present rejoicing while suffering.

Don't place your hope in favorable circumstances, which won't last. Place your hope in Christ and his promises.

> "It may be said with certainty that Christians who have lost their enthusiasm about the Savior's promises of Heaven-to-come have also stopped being effective in Christian life and witness in this world."
>
> A.W. Tozer

O God, you are my God; earnestly I seek you;
my soul thirsts for you;
my flesh faints for you,
as in a dry and weary land
where there is no water.

PSALM 63:1 ESV

In a fallen world, people keep searching, like frustrated channel changers, never finding what satisfies. Ultimate satisfaction is found only in Jesus. We're made for him and we'll never be satisfied with less.

Because we're made for greatness, the world's superficiality is unsatisfying. We sense dissatisfaction is abnormal, and we ache for someone, somehow, to bring us contentment. The someone is Jesus, and the somehow is his redemptive work.

"Mankind intuitively places their hopes and allegiance in a perceived great one. We want someone we can look up to, believe in, and identify with. Image-bearers need a hero. More specifically, fallen humanity needs a Savior. All the beauty longings of our heart scream for just one beauty that restores, fulfills, and endures. Christianity heralds just such a beautiful one: Jesus Christ."

Steve DeWitt

But nothing unclean will ever enter [the city], nor anyone who does what is detestable or false, but only those who are written in the Lamb's book of life.
REVELATION 21:27 ESV

Judging by most funerals, you'd think nearly *everyone's* going to Heaven. But Jesus said, "Small is the gate and narrow the road that leads to life, and only a few find it" (Matthew 7:14).

In Bible times cities kept lists of their residents. Guards were at the gates to keep out enemies by checking the list. Revelation 21 explains how Heaven will be like those cities. Jesus has the "book of life," which lists the names of his followers, who will live with him in Heaven.

We have not written our names in Heaven—*God* has. That God chose us, despite our unworthiness, is the greatest reason to celebrate.

> "When God writes our names in the 'Lamb's Book of Life,' he doesn't do it with an eraser handy. He does it for eternity."
>
> *R.C. Sproul*

Therefore judge nothing before the appointed time;
wait until the Lord comes. He will bring to light
what is hidden in darkness and will expose the
motives of the heart. At that time each will receive
their praise from God.

1 CORINTHIANS 4:5

All people should live each day with this awesome awareness: "But they will have to give account to him who is
ready to judge the living and the dead" (1 Peter 4:5).

We're all sinners, and the wages of sin is death (Romans
6:23). But a holy God, out of love for us, judged Jesus for
our sins. Only by embracing Christ's atonement for our
sins can we escape everlasting punishment. God's justice
was satisfied, but at the cost of his own blood.

We'll all meet Jesus when we die. If we're ready, we'll
long for his return. If we aren't, we'll dread it. Now is the
time to get ready.

"There is more mercy in Christ than sin in us."

Richard Sibbes

My desire is to depart and be with Christ,
for that is far better.
PHILIPPIANS 1:23 ESV

Paul could have said, "I desire to depart and be in Heaven," but he didn't. Being with Jesus is the most significant aspect of Heaven.

Every other heavenly pleasure will derive from and be secondary to his presence, the heart and soul of Heaven. God's greatest gift will always be himself.

Samuel Rutherford said: "O my Lord Jesus Christ, if I could be in Heaven without thee, it would be a Hell; and if I could be in Hell, and have thee still, it would be a Heaven to me, for thou art all the Heaven I want."

A place with Christ cannot be Hell, only Heaven. A place without Christ cannot be Heaven, only Hell.

"Heaven isn't a place for people who are scared of Hell; it's for people who love Jesus. The reason Heaven is heavenly—full of joy, life, and bliss—is because we'll be with Jesus."

Jefferson Bethke

*There is no fear in love. But perfect love drives out
fear, because fear has to do with punishment.
The one who fears is not made perfect in love.
We love because he first loved us.*

1 JOHN 4:18-19

In Heaven we'll worship Jesus as the Almighty and bow to him in reverence, yet we'll never sense his disapproval—because we'll never disappoint him. He'll never be unhappy with us. We'll be able to relax in Heaven.

Jesus bore all our sins, removing our condemnation and considering us innocent, declaring us righteous. We're as acceptable to the Father as Christ himself, with no barriers between us and him. God is totally and irreversibly satisfied with us because he is totally and irreversibly satisfied with Christ's work on our behalf.

"At the cross in holy love God through Christ paid the full penalty of our disobedience himself. He bore the judgment we deserve in order to bring us the forgiveness we do not deserve."

John Stott

> *[Simeon] took him up in his arms and blessed*
> *God and said, "Lord, now you are letting your*
> *servant depart in peace...for my eyes have seen your*
> *salvation that you have prepared in the presence of*
> *all peoples, a light for revelation to the Gentiles, and*
> *for glory to your people Israel."*
> LUKE 2:28-32 ESV

God promised Simeon, a "righteous and devout" old man living in Jerusalem at the time of Christ's birth, that he wouldn't die until he had seen the Messiah. The culminating joy of Simeon's life was to see Jesus when he was brought to the temple.

We too have been promised that we'll see Jesus. As Simeon lived his earthly life in anticipation of seeing Jesus, so should we. All else—in this world and the next—will be secondary to beholding our Lord. To see Jesus—what could be greater?

"Because the face of God is so lovely...so beautiful, once you have seen it, nothing else can give you pleasure. It will give insatiable satisfaction of which we will never tire."

Augustine

180

*"Anyone who loves their father or mother more
than me is not worthy of me."*
MATTHEW 10:37

Christ put himself before the human authorities of family
(Matthew 10:21-22) and government (Matthew 22:15-22).
Even the church can end up putting man's authority before
God's.

When asked about paying taxes, Jesus said, "Give
back to Caesar what is Caesar's, and to God what is God's"
(Matthew 22:21). The first half of his statement answered
the question, but the second half put Caesar in his place.
For whoever Caesar may be, he's *not* God.

When the Sanhedrin told them not to preach the gospel, Peter and the apostles did so anyway. They said, "We
must obey God rather than human beings!" (Acts 5:29).
It's obedience to *God's* commandments that is the focus of
Scripture from beginning to end.

> "If you do not plan to live the Christian life totally
> committed to knowing your God and to walking in
> obedience to him, then don't begin, for this is what
> Christianity is all about."
>
> *Kay Arthur*

Since we have confidence to enter the Most Holy Place by the blood of Jesus...let us draw near to God with a sincere heart and with the full assurance that faith brings.

HEBREWS 10:19,22

To be welcomed into the presence of our Lord—this is the wonder of our redemption. Though we can't experience its fullness yet, we can gain a foretaste now.

We shouldn't read these verses casually, for they tell us something wonderful beyond comprehension—that the blood of Jesus has bought us full access to God's throne room (Hebrews 4:16) and his "Most Holy Place." Unlike the Israelites, we can freely come into his presence, thanks to Jesus.

He welcomes us to come there in prayer now. And in eternity he'll also welcome us to live in his presence as resurrected beings.

"I bless thee for the throne of grace, that here free favour reigns; that open access to it is through the blood of Jesus."

Puritan Prayer

182

> *"Be dressed ready for service...like servants waiting
> for their master to return...so that when he comes
> and knocks they can immediately open the door for
> him. It will be good for those servants whose master
> finds them watching when he comes. Truly I tell you,
> he will dress himself to serve, will have them recline
> at the table and will come and wait on them."*
> LUKE 12:35-37

Matthew 20:28 says, "The Son of Man did not come to
be served, but to serve, and to give his life as a ransom for
many." Jesus modeled servant leadership in his life and
death. He said his servants who are ready and waiting for
his return will be rewarded, and *he* will serve them.

Imagine being served by Jesus! We owe him everything. He owes us nothing. But that doesn't keep God
from choosing to serve us.

> "It is relatively easy to serve those above us—
> even the world expects this—but Jesus served
> downward."
>
> *Jerry Bridges*

*"Therefore you also must be ready, for the Son of Man
is coming at an hour you do not expect."*
MATTHEW 24:44 ESV

When will Christ return? Believers have been speculating ever since his ascension.

We should believe in the imminent return of Christ, which means he *can* return any time. But it also means he doesn't *have to* return anytime soon.

Instead of speculating, we should focus on what the Bible has told us all along—fear God, trust God, be faithful, be generous, care for your family, look after the body of Christ, and reach out to unbelievers.

Let's shine the light as faithful children of God. Let's trust Jesus to return when he's good and ready. Let's live as people who are going to meet Jesus soon, either by his return or by our deaths.

> "We are to wait for the coming of Christ with patience. We are to watch with anticipation. We are to work with zeal. We are to prepare with urgency."
>
> *Billy Graham*

184

The angel said to the women, "Do not be afraid, for I know that you are looking for Jesus, who was crucified. He is not here; he has risen, just as he said."

MATTHEW 28:5-6

Jesus said, "Destroy this temple, and I will raise it again in three days" (John 2:19). John clarifies that "the temple he had spoken of was his body" (v. 21).

The empty tomb is absolute proof that Christ's resurrection body was the same body that died on the cross. If resurrection meant the creation of a new body, Christ's original body would have remained in the tomb. Jesus said to his disciples after his resurrection, "It is I myself," emphasizing he was the same person—in spirit and body—who was crucified.

Christ's resurrection body was really his, the same one since conception. Ours will actually be ours, never again to suffer deterioration, disease, or death.

"There is a one-to-one correspondence between the body of Christ that died and the body that rose."

Hank Hanegraaff

185

*Jesus himself stood among them and said to them,
"Peace be with you." They were startled and
frightened, thinking they saw a ghost. He said to
them, "Why are you troubled...? Look at my hands
and my feet. It is I myself! Touch me and see; a ghost
does not have flesh and bones, as you see I have."*
LUKE 24:36-39

Strangely, though Jesus in his resurrected body proclaimed,
"I am not a ghost" (Luke 24:39 NLT), countless Christians
think they will be ghosts or disembodied spirits in Heaven.
The magnificent, cosmos-shaking victory of Christ's resurrection—by definition a physical triumph over physical
death in a physical world—escapes them. If Jesus had been
a ghost, if *we* would be ghosts, then *redemption wouldn't
have been accomplished.*

Jesus walked the Earth in his resurrection body for
forty days, showing us how we would live as resurrected
human beings.

"The bodily resurrection of Jesus Christ from the
dead is the crowning proof of Christianity."

Henry Morris

"I know that my redeemer lives,
and that in the end he will stand on the earth.
And after my skin has been destroyed,
yet in my flesh I will see God;
I myself will see him with my own eyes—
I, and not another.
How my heart yearns within me!"
JOB 19:25-27

In the midst of bone-crushing anguish, Job cried out that his Redeemer would one day come to Earth. And even though Job's body would be destroyed through physical death, he knew he would in his own flesh see God. What a clear reference to the coming resurrection.

Jesus will be a human being for all eternity, and we'll know him as *both* God and man. To not only worship God but to also see God, run alongside God, play catch with God…that's about as stunning a truth as there is.

"Veiled in flesh the Godhead see,
Hail the incarnate Deity!
Pleased as man with men to dwell,
Jesus, our Emmanuel."

Charles Wesley

187

Of the increase of his government and of
peace there will be no end,
on the throne of David and over his kingdom,
to establish it and to uphold it with justice
and with righteousness
from this time forth and forevermore.

ISAIAH 9:7 ESV

Some Christians err by ignoring politics, failing to exercise God-given stewardship. Others put too much confidence in politics, failing to understand that no political philosophy redeems us—only Jesus does. God alone will establish a perfect government on Earth.

When have we ever experienced the "peace on Earth" promised at Christ's birth? We haven't yet, but we will (Zechariah 9:9-10). Meanwhile, God calls us to cultural reform. Christians can do much good in politics, but we shouldn't forget that the only government that will succeed in global reform is Christ's.

"The boundless realms of his Father's universe are Christ's by prescriptive right. As 'heir of all things,' he is the sole proprietor of the vast creation of God, and he has admitted us."

Charles Spurgeon

> *"In the time of those kings, the God of heaven will set up a kingdom that will never be destroyed, nor will it be left to another people. It will crush all those kingdoms and bring them to an end, but it will itself endure forever."*
>
> DANIEL 2:44

Human kingdoms will rise and fall until Christ brings to Earth a Kingdom where mankind will rule in righteousness (Luke 22:29-30; 2 Timothy 2:12). As Christ will be the King of kings, his realm will be the Kingdom of kingdoms—the greatest kingdom in human history. Yes, human history, for our history will not end at Christ's return or upon our relocation to the New Earth; it will continue forever, to the glory of God.

> "If our hearts should fail us as we stand over against the hosts of wickedness which surround us, let us encourage ourselves and one another with the great reminder: Remember Jesus Christ, risen from the dead, of the seed of David!"
>
> *B.B. Warfield*

> *When I saw him, I fell at his feet as though dead.*
> *Then he placed his right hand on me and said:*
> *"Do not be afraid. I am the First and the Last."*
>
> REVELATION 1:17

Everything good, enjoyable, and refreshing derives from God. The joys of Heaven will overflow from his multifaceted wonders.

Heaven will be endlessly fascinating, just like Jesus, who is anything *but* boring. Seeing God will be dynamic, not static. It'll mean exploring new beauties, unfolding new mysteries—forever. If this were all there is to Heaven, it would be enough.

John was Christ's dearest friend on Earth. But seeing Jesus in Heaven, he "fell at his feet as though dead." One day we'll see Christ in his glory. The most exhilarating experiences on Earth won't begin to compare with the thrill of seeing Jesus.

"As there is nothing greater or better than God himself…God shall be the end of all our desires, who will be seen without end, loved without cloy, and praised without weariness."

Augustine

*And God raised us up with Christ and seated us
with him in the heavenly realms in Christ Jesus,
in order that in the coming ages he might show the
incomparable riches of his grace, expressed in his
kindness to us in Christ Jesus.*

EPHESIANS 2:6-7

We will never stop learning about Christ and his qualities
and affection for us. This will be a progressive, ongoing
revelation in which we learn more and more about God's
grace and kindness in Christ.

Samuel Rutherford wrote, "Every day we may see
some new thing in Christ. His love has neither brim nor
bottom."

I often learn new things about my family and closest
friends though I've known them for many years. If I can
always be learning something new about finite, limited
human beings, how much more will I be learning about
Jesus in the ages to come? None of us will ever begin to
exhaust his depths.

"The loveliness of Christ is fresh to all eternity."

John Flavel

"Blessed are the pure in heart, for they will see God."
MATTHEW 5:8

We think the universe revolves around us. We have to remind ourselves it's all about Christ, not us. In Heaven we'll never have to correct our thinking. Tony Reinke writes, "We are distracted by our self-focus. All our boasting and pompous self-talk would be so utterly vain if we were to see Christ fully with our eyes of faith."

Because in Heaven our hearts will be pure and we'll see people as they truly are, every relationship will be pure. We'll all be faithful to the love of our life: King Jesus.

We'll love everyone, but we'll be *in* love only with Jesus. We'll never believe the outrageous lie that our deepest needs can be met in anyone but Jesus.

> "What shall we do in heaven?…Worship, work, think, and communicate, enjoying activity, beauty, people, and God. First and foremost, however, we shall see and love Jesus, our Savior, Master, and Friend."
>
> J.I. Packer

Jesus did many other things as well. If every one of them were written down, I suppose that even the whole world would not have room for the books that would be written.

JOHN 21:25

The Gospels contain wonderful stories. How much more will there be to tell about Jesus' never-ending life with his people on the New Earth? We can look forward to endless adventures and delightful experiences with him.

Imagine the stories Jesus will tell us when we're in his presence: about creating the world and distant galaxies, what the universe is like, about making the first dinosaur, or becoming a baby—we'll all be on the edge of our seats.

Of course, the greatest story ever told will be permanently engraved in the hands and feet of Jesus. That story, above all, will be in our hearts and on our tongues.

> "I love to tell the story,
>   'Twill be my theme in glory
>   To tell the old, old story
>   of Jesus and his love."
>
> *Katherine Hankey*

193

The shepherds said to one another, "Let's go to Bethlehem and see this thing that has happened, which the Lord has told us about."

LUKE 2:15

In Jesus' day, shepherds were officially labeled "sinners"—a technical term for a class of despised people. Yet, it was the sinners, not the self-righteous, he came to save (Mark 2:17).

Into this social context of religious snobbery and class prejudice, God's Son stepped forth. How surprising and significant that God handpicked unpretentious shepherds to first hear the joyous news: "It's a boy, the Messiah!"

The image of the shepherd was immortalized by Jesus when he said, "I am the good shepherd" (John 10:11). No other illustration so vividly portrays his tender care and guiding hand.

> "God is not ashamed of the lowliness of human beings…He chooses people as his instruments and performs his wonders where one would least expect them. God is near to lowliness; he loves the lost, the neglected, the unseemly, the excluded, the weak and broken."
>
> *Dietrich Bonhoeffer*

Rejoice greatly, Daughter Zion!
Shout, Daughter Jerusalem!
See, your king comes to you, righteous and victorious,
lowly and riding on a donkey...
He will proclaim peace to the nations.
His rule will extend from sea to sea and from the
River to the ends of the earth.
ZECHARIAH 9:9-10

Matthew 21:5 quotes this passage in reference to the Messiah. Just as the first part of the prophecy was literally fulfilled when Jesus rode a donkey into Jerusalem, we should expect the second part will be literally fulfilled as well.

We're promised that "the LORD will be king over the whole earth" (Zechariah 14:9). Bible-believing Jews were wrong about the Messiah's identity when they rejected Christ, and wrong to overlook his need to come as a suffering servant to redeem the world.

But they were *right* to believe the Messiah would forever rule the Earth. He will!

"Rejoice, the Lord is King!
Your Lord and King adore;
Rejoice, give thanks, and sing,
And triumph evermore."
Charles Wesley

God has now revealed to us his mysterious will
regarding Christ…At the right time he will bring
everything together under the authority of Christ—
everything in heaven and on earth.
EPHESIANS 1:9-10 NLT

God's plan of the ages is to bring everything in Heaven and on Earth together under Christ. "Everything" is all inclusive—meaning nothing left out. As Ephesians 1:10 demonstrates, Earth and Heaven becoming one is explicitly biblical. There'll be one universe, with all things in Heaven and on Earth together under one head, Jesus Christ.

The hymn "This Is My Father's World" expresses this truth: "Jesus who died shall be satisfied, and Earth and Heaven be one." Just as God and mankind are reconciled in Christ, so the dwellings of God and mankind—Heaven and Earth—will be reconciled in Christ. Affirming anything less understates the redemptive work of Christ.

"Christianity must yet triumph in a renovated earth,
and with the returned Messiah as universal king, or
fail. There is no third alternative."

Anthony Buzzard

196

*"My dwelling place will be with them; I will be their
God, and they will be my people."*

Ezekiel 37:27

Heaven is God's home. Earth is ours. Jesus, as the God-
man, forever links God and mankind, and thereby forever links Heaven and Earth. Christ will make Earth into
Heaven and Heaven into Earth.

The angel promised Mary concerning Jesus, "The
Lord God will give him the throne of his father David,
and he will reign over Jacob's descendants forever" (Luke
1:32-33). David's throne isn't in Heaven but on Earth. It's
God's reign on Earth, not in Heaven, that's the focus of the
unfolding drama of redemption.

There will be one cosmos, one universe united under
one Lord—forever. This is the unstoppable plan of God.
This is where history is headed.

> "'God with us' is eternity's sonnet, Heaven's halle-
> lujah, the shout of the glorified, the song of the
> redeemed, the chorus of the angels, the everlasting
> oratorio of the great orchestra of the sky."
>
> *Charles Spurgeon*

"See, your Savior comes!
See, his reward is with him,
and his recompense accompanies him."
ISAIAH 62:11

Jesus says to Christians, "I am he who searches hearts and minds, and I will repay each of you according to your deeds" (Revelation 2:23).

If we're his children, God is for us, not against us (Romans 8:31). He's assured us our names are written in the Book of Life. He wants to commend and reward us at the judgment seat of Christ. He doesn't want the faithful works of our lifetime forgotten. He wants us to have eternal rewards—and he's given us every resource we need in Christ to live the godly life, resulting in those rewards (2 Peter 1:3).

Christ-centered righteous living today is directly affected by knowing where we're going and what rewards we'll receive for serving Christ.

"Let us remember, there is One who daily records all we do for him, and sees more beauty in his servants' work than his servants do themselves."

J.C. Ryle

*The nursing child shall play over
the hole of the cobra,
and the weaned child shall put his
hand on the adder's den.*

ISAIAH 11:8 ESV

God promises we'll one day play with animals that are now dangerous. Since he's the creator of play and wired his image-bearers and even animals to enjoy play, we know that Jesus must have played—after all, he was once a child!

God describes children playing as a fruit of his presence. He promises a time of great happiness: "The city streets will be filled with boys and girls playing there" (Zechariah 8:5). What a beautiful and hope-giving picture! Play is part of a perfect world.

What will it be like for people and animals to play with the One who made them to love play? Nothing short of glorious.

"The beloved Son of God is [the Father's] most precious treasure, in which God's infinite riches, and infinite happiness and joy, from eternity to eternity, does consist."

Jonathan Edwards

> *"Take up my yoke and learn from me, because
> I am lowly and humble in heart, and you
> will find rest for your souls."*
> MATTHEW 11:29 CSB

Jesus said to his disciples, "Learn from me." There's such joy in learning when the subject matter is fascinating and the teacher is captivating. On the New Earth, we'll have the privilege of sitting at Jesus' feet and learning from him.

Even now, time spent at his feet is an investment in eternity, a treasure stored in Heaven. We can learn from Christ by going to him in prayer, meditating upon him, asking him for help, and spending time in his Word.

"My sheep listen to my voice," Jesus said (John 10:27). Have you been listening to his voice lately?

> "Get into God's Word, and you will get a heart for Jesus. Get passionate about Scripture, and your passion for him will increase. Feelings follow faith... and faith comes by hearing, and hearing by the Word of God."
>
> *Joni Eareckson Tada*

*For God so loved the world that he gave his
one and only Son, that whoever believes in him
shall not perish but have eternal life.*

JOHN 3:16

E. Stanley Jones, in his book *Abundant Living*, observed, "The early Christians did not say in dismay, 'look what the world has come to,' but in delight, 'look what has come into the world.'"

"What has come" is Jesus Christ, a person so attractive, so magnetic, and so joyful that he changed the world not only by his death but also by his life.

I think we'll celebrate the incarnation of Christ for all eternity. The thrill of being in his presence will never wear off, and the adventures ahead of us will always be better than the ones behind.

> "It won't be long before your faith will be rewarded with the sight of the One who has promised to be with you to the end."
>
> *Nancy DeMoss Wolgemuth*

Conclusion

Anticipating Seeing Jesus Face to Face and Living with Him Forever

Though Genesis 3:8 follows after the first sin, it describes a situation I think was a regular part of God's relationship with Adam and Eve before their fall: "The man and his wife heard the sound of the LORD God as he was walking in the garden in the cool of the day."

This is what we were made for: fellowship with God, enjoying his company and the warmth of his love, worshiping him wholeheartedly in the midst of his creation. This is why sin has left everyone so hollow, such a shell of what we once were. Adam and Eve regularly *saw God*, and he was their delight.

All that changed after the Fall.

Holy, Unapproachable God

When Moses said to God, "Show me your glory," God responded, "I will cause all my goodness to pass in front of you…[But] you cannot see my face, for no one may see me and live…When my glory passes by, I will put you in a cleft in the rock and cover you with my hand until I have passed by. Then I will remove my hand and you will see my back; but my face must not be seen" (Exodus 33:18-23).

Moses saw God, but not God's face. Yet in another

sense "the Lord would speak to Moses face to face, as one speaks to a friend" (Exodus 33:11).

The New Testament says that God "lives in unapproachable light, whom no one has seen or can see" (1 Timothy 6:16).

Sinful humans are rightly terrified by the prospect of seeing God. Consider Samson's father, Manoah, who after seeing the angel of the Lord, told his wife, "We are doomed to die! We have seen God!" (Judges 13:22).

Yet Job cried out with this ancient hope and solid confidence:

> "I know that my redeemer lives,
>   and that in the end he will stand on the earth.
> And after my skin has been destroyed,
>   yet in my flesh I will see God;
> I myself will see him
>   with my own eyes—I and not another.
>   *How my heart yearns within me!*"
>
>   (Job 19:25-27)

David, too, longed to be where God was and to gaze on his beauty. He wrote,

> One thing I ask from the Lord,
>   this only do I seek:
> that I may dwell in the house of the Lord
>   all the days of my life,

to gaze on the beauty of the LORD
and to seek him in his temple.

(PSALM 27:4)

But to actually *see* God? Before the incarnation, such a desire seemed unthinkable.

Jesus, God Made Approachable

The God who lives in unapproachable light became approachable in the person of Jesus (John 1:14). In fact, it was Jesus himself who made God visible to us: "No one has ever seen God, but the one and only Son, who is himself God and is in closest relationship with the Father, has made him known" (John 1:18).

Consider the dialogue between Philip and Jesus in John 14:8-9:

Philip said, "Lord, show us the Father and that will be enough for us."

Jesus answered: "Don't you know me, Philip, even after I have been among you such a long time? *Anyone who has seen me has seen the Father.* How can you say, 'Show us the Father'?"

Jesus also says, "Blessed are the pure in heart, for they will see God" (Matthew 5:8). This is all a precursor to what God promises we'll experience after the resurrection, on the New Earth: "No longer will there be any curse. The throne of God and of the Lamb will be in the city, and his servants will serve him. *They will see his face*" (Revelation 22:3-4).

"Without holiness no one will see the Lord" (Hebrews 12:14). For us to see God would require us to undergo radical transformation between now and then. And that's exactly what will happen. By faith in Christ, God's children already have his righteousness, which will allow us into Heaven (Romans 3:22; 2 Corinthians 5:21). Because we stand completely righteous before God in Christ, once we're glorified and forever made sinless, we'll be able to see God and live. Though we will always be creature and he Creator, in Heaven we'll be able to actually see his face. We will experience the answer to the psalmist David's prayer.

Incredible.

English poet John Donne (1572–1631) wrote beautifully of this coming day for every child of God: "I shall rise from the dead...I shall see the Son of God, the sun of Glory, and shine myself, as that sun shines. I shall...be united to the Ancient of Days, to God himself, who had no morning, never began." He also said, "No man ever saw God and lived; and yet, I shall not live till I see God; and when I have seen him I shall never die."

Do you sense the happiness and wonder in Donne's words?

The Happiest-Making Sight

Ancient theologians often spoke of the "beatific vision."

The term comes from three Latin words that together mean "a happy-making sight." The sight they spoke of was God. To see God's face is the loftiest of all aspirations. But sadly, for most of us, it's not at the top of our list of desires.

Wayne Grudem writes in his *Systematic Theology*:

> When we look into the face of our Lord and he looks back at us with infinite love, we will see in him the fulfillment of everything that we know to be good and right and desirable in the universe. In the face of God we will see the fulfillment of all the longing we have ever had to know perfect love, peace, and joy, and to know truth and justice, holiness and wisdom, goodness and power, and glory and beauty.

The most astonishing sight we can anticipate in Heaven is not streets of gold or pearly gates or loved ones who've died before us. It will be coming face-to-face with our Savior. To look into Jesus' eyes will be to see what we've always longed to see: the *person* who made us and for whom we were made. And we'll see him in the *place* he made for us and for which we were made. Seeing God will be like seeing everything else for the first time.

I sometimes ponder what it'll be like to see Jesus, to fall on my knees before him, then talk with him and eat with him and walk with him as a resurrected person living on a resurrected Earth. Like Job I'm struck with the realization that "I myself will see him with my own eyes—I, and not another. How my heart yearns within me!"

I try to picture what this will be like in my novel *Edge of Eternity*, when the main character, Nick Seagrave, at last gazes on Jesus Christ:

> The King stepped from the great city, just outside the gate, and put his hand on my shoulder. I was aware of no one and nothing but him. I saw before me an aged, weathered King, thoughtful guardian of an empire. But I also saw a virile Warrior-Prince primed for battle, eager to mount his steed and march in conquest. His eyes were keen as sharpened swords yet deep as wells, full of the memories of the old and the dreams of the young.

Shut your eyes and imagine seeing Jesus for the first time. What a wondrous thought! And what a wondrous promise!

Meanwhile, let's devote our lives to getting to know this Savior, in anticipation of one day seeing his face. By studying his words and character, we can prepare for the day when we'll at last gaze on him and say, "Yes! This is the One who I saw in his Word before, and now see perfectly!"

Seeing the face of Christ, we'll spend the coming ages learning more and more of his grace and kindness.

I can hardly wait!

How about you?

WHAT NEXT?

You may wish to reread this book and meditate on or memorize the Scriptures at its core. You might want to share it with a friend or discuss it with a group. If you're not part of a community of believers who are learning the truths of God's Word, find a Jesus-centered, Bible-teaching church. (If you need help locating one in your area, contact our ministry at info@epm.org and we will assist you.)

There is no better place to learn about Jesus than in the four Gospels: Matthew, Mark, Luke, and John. There's also much about him in the New Testament letters and the book of Revelation, as well as various portions of the Old Testament.

Here are other Jesus-related books you may find helpful:

- *The Incomparable Christ*, John Stott
- *Seeing and Savoring Jesus Christ*, John Piper
- *The Case for Christ*, Lee Strobel
- *The Jesus I Never Knew*, Philip Yancey
- *The Man Christ Jesus*, Bruce Ware
- *Who Is This Man?*, John Ortberg
- *Jesus the King: Understanding the Life and Death of the Son of God*, Timothy Keller

- *Encounters with Jesus*, Timothy Keller
- *More Than a Carpenter*, Josh McDowell
- *Sitting at the Feet of Rabbi Jesus*, Ann Spangler and Lois Tverberg
- *Jesus: The Greatest Life of All*, Charles R. Swindoll
- *The First Days of Jesus*, Andreas J. Köstenberger, Alexander Stewart, and Justin Taylor
- *The Final Days of Jesus*, Andreas J. Köstenberger, Alexander Stewart, and Justin Taylor
- *Jesus Among Secular Gods: The Countercultural Claims of Christ*, Ravi Zacharias
- *The Jesus Storybook Bible: Every Story Whispers His Name*, Sally Lloyd-Jones
- *Jesus and the Victory of God*, N.T. Wright
- *Simply Jesus: A New Vision of Who He Was, What He Did, and Why He Matters*, N.T. Wright
- *The Book of Jesus: A Treasury of the Greatest Stories and Writings About Christ*, Calvin Miller
- *The Incomparable Christ*, J. Oswald Sanders, J.I. Packer (Foreword)

Scripture Quotation Sources

About the Author

Randy is the founder and director of Eternal Perspective Ministries, which began in 1990. Previously he served as a pastor for fourteen years. He has a bachelor of theology and a master of arts in biblical studies degrees from Multnomah University and an honorary doctorate from Western Seminary in Portland, Oregon. He has taught on the adjunct faculties of both.

A *New York Times* bestselling author, Randy has written over fifty books, including *Happiness*, *Heaven* (over one million sold), *The Treasure Principle* (over two million sold), *If God Is Good*, and *Safely Home* (winner of the Gold Medallion award for fiction). His books have been translated into more than seventy languages and have sold ten million copies. Randy has written for many magazines including EPM's *Eternal Perspectives*. He blogs, is active daily on Facebook and Twitter, and has been a guest on more than eight hundred radio, television, and online programs.

Randy resides in Gresham, Oregon, with his wife, Nanci. They have two married daughters and are the proud grandparents of five grandsons. Randy enjoys hanging out with his family, biking, underwater photography, research, and reading.

Contact Eternal Perspective Ministries at www.epm.org or 39085 Pioneer Blvd., Suite 206, Sandy, OR 97055 or 503.668.5200. Follow Randy on Facebook: www.facebook.com/randyalcorn; Twitter: www.twitter.com/randy-alcorn; and on his blog: www.epm.org/blog.

To learn more about Harvest House books and
to read sample chapters, visit our website:

www.harvesthousepublishers.com

HARVEST HOUSE PUBLISHERS
EUGENE, OREGON